CORE SKILLS

Reading
Comprehension

Martha K. Resnick
Carolyn J. Hyatt
Sylvia E. Freiman

Harcourt Achieve

Rigby • Steck-Vaughn

www.HarcourtAchieve.com
1.800.531.5015

About the Authors

Martha K. Resnick is an experienced elementary teacher, formerly a Reading Resource Teacher with the Baltimore City Schools. She has served as a cooperative practice teacher, training student teachers from many colleges. Mrs. Resnick received her master's degree in education at Loyola College.

Carolyn J. Hyatt has taught elementary, secondary, and adult education classes. She was formerly a Senior Teacher with the Baltimore City Schools. Mrs. Hyatt received her master's degree in education at Loyola College.

Sylvia E. Freiman has taught primary and upper elementary grades. She has conducted teacher in-service classes, supervised student teachers, and participated in curriculum planning. Mrs. Freiman received her master's degree in education at Johns Hopkins University.

Acknowledgments

Designer: Rusty Kaim
Media Researcher: Sarah Fraser
Cover Design: Alexandra Corona
Interior Illustrations: Don Collins, David Cunningham, Rosemarie Fox-Hicks, and Don Sibley
Photography: p. 61 (left) © Ted Farrington/Root Resources; p. 61 (right) © Stan Osolinski/Root Resources; p. 94 North Wind Picture Archives
Composition: The Clarinda Company

ISBN 978-0-7398-5734-2
ISBN 0-7398-5734-7
Copyright © 2002 Harcourt Achieve Inc.

14   0868 12   4500348035

Dear Parent,

Welcome to the *Steck-Vaughn Core Skills: Reading Comprehension* series! You have selected a unique book that focuses on developing your child's comprehension skills, the reading and thinking processes associated with the printed word. Because this series was designed by experienced reading professionals, your child will have reading success as well as gain a firm understanding of the necessary skills outlined in national standards.

Reading should be a fun, relaxed activity for children. They should read stories that relate to or build on their own experiences. Vocabulary should be presented in a sequential and logical progression. The stories in this series build on these philosophies to insure your child's reading success. Other important features in this series that will further aid your child include:

- Short reading selections of interest to a young reader.

- Vocabulary introduced in context and repeated often.

- Comprehension skills applied in context to make the reading more relevant.

- Multiple choice exercises that develop skills for standardized test taking.

You may wish to have your child read the selections silently or orally, but you will find that sharing the stories and activities with your child will provide additional confidence and support to succeed. When learners experience success, learning becomes a continuous process moving them onward to higher achievements. Moreover, the more your child reads, the more proficient she or he will become.

Enjoy this special time with your child!

Sincerely,
The Educators and Staff of
Steck-Vaughn School Supply

P.S. You might also like to visit the Special Features section of our website at **www.svschoolsupply.com** for other fun activities and learning suggestions.

Contents

Correlation to Language Arts Content Standards

LANGUAGE ARTS SKILLS	PAGE
Comprehension	
Cause and Effect	105
Drawing Conclusions	104, 120
Fact or Fiction	109, 110, 115, 116, 117, 122
Facts and Inferences	9, 10, 14, 27, 28, 36, 38, 39, 43, 44, 57, 58, 69, 70, 78, 79, 103, 111
Graphic Sources	22, 30, 31, 37, 53, 54, 72, 98, 99
Main Ideas and Supporting Details	36, 37, 38, 39, 45, 46, 47, 48, 49, 50, 59, 60, 61, 62, 63
Predicting	11
Relevant and Irrelevant Information	31, 117, 118, 121
Sequencing	30, 31, 54, 72
Vocabulary	
Analogies	80, 99
Antonyms	28, 54
Multiple Meanings	61, 79, 92
Synonyms	58, 59
Word Meaning	10, 15, 40, 71, 72, 90, 91, 106
Words in Context	29, 114, 119
Research and Study Skills	
Encyclopedia	87
Evaluating Persuasive Methods	112, 113, 119
Evaluating Resources	86, 87, 88, 93, 117, 118, 121
Outlining	16, 17, 18, 19, 20, 21, 51, 52, 95, 96, 97
Parts of a Book	88, 89, 94, 95
Skimming	36, 37, 49, 50, 72

It was very early in the morning. Binoculars in hand, Brenda walked noiselessly along the trails and dales in Burton Woods. Suddenly she stopped. Could that be a yellow-bellied sapsucker half-hidden in the branches above her? The other bird-watchers in the group paused when Brenda did. Simultaneously, all of them raised their binoculars to their eyes.

An air of quiet excitement swept the group as they glimpsed the rare woodpecker. The most conscientious bird-watchers recorded the date, location, and time of the sighting.

Brenda turned her binoculars on some people camped along a trail farther down the slope. The campers were sitting by their campfire, flipping pancakes and boiling coffee.

Brenda stiffened. "I hope they remember to shovel dirt on those ashes and stamp out every ember," she thought. "They built that fire in a bad place, too, near those fallen tree trunks."

The lovely, bright summer day on the trails was spoiled for Brenda. Although she was just twelve years old, Brenda had experienced two huge fires. Her experience had left her with a terrible fear of flames. Now she was very aware of the danger of fires caused by careless campers.

Scenes of the conflagration in Yellowstone Park in 1988 and the inferno that destroyed her grandparents' home in Oakland, California, in 1991 flashed through Brenda's mind. Brenda had been in both places. Since then she had read much about forest fires and had become very knowledgeable about them.

The fire in Yellowstone Park was started by lightning. It was first noticed when campers and visitors saw smoke in the sky. It seemed to be far away. Brenda, her parents, and her three brothers were some of the campers. They were shocked when a strong wind suddenly swept the fire through the dry bushes and underbrush. It started roaring not far from their tents. Lack of rain had made the dry wooded area very flammable. The dry wood and underbrush ignited easily from sparks. The Yellowstone forest rangers announced that everyone must evacuate the campsites by seven the next morning, July 23.

The rangers used chain saws to cut down all the trees close to buildings and hauled away all the dead wood and fallen branches. They tried to make a clearing around the buildings that would serve as a firebreak. With no wood or dry material to feed on, the flames might turn in another direction.

Brenda's older brothers, Abner and Josh, eagerly volunteered to help the rangers. Their offers were firmly, but politely, turned down. They were directed to move out. Brenda was relieved when her whole family drove down the smoky road from their campsite to safety far from the crackling flames.

Eight huge fires burned at once in Yellowstone Park. In one area, there were thousands of dry, dead lodgepole pine trees that made the perfect fuel for the growling, crackling flames. The trees had been killed by beetles boring into them, and now quickly became engulfed by fire. While they blazed, sparks and embers from the conflagration spread to the live pine trees nearby, destroying them, too.

A wide, paved highway through the wilderness usually served as a firebreak, but in the lodgepole pine forest the road and nearby parking lots only caused the fire to pause. Fifty-mile-an-hour winds pushed the flame across the cleared space to the other side.

The Yellowstone fires continued to burn all through August and into September. The flames came closer and closer to Old Faithful, the park's most famous geyser.

Many more firefighters were brought in. Their trucks drove as close to the conflagration as possible. Men and women dressed in green-and-yellow fire-retardant uniforms got out and started to work. They dug a fire line by hand. They toiled in heat and smoke, digging down to the bare rock. There would be nothing for the fire to feed on.

The huge blazes were also fought by helicopters. The pilots lowered buckets into lakes and ponds and pulled up water. Then they flew over the places where the sparks and embers were beginning to catch hold on dry leaves and wood and start new fires. The helicopters doused them with water to extinguish the flames. Airplanes also sprayed water down to wet the vegetation and keep the flames at bay.

All firefighters in the wilderness are required to have fire shelters clipped to their belts. Fire shelters are fire-retardant bags which can be placed all around the head and body. They are used if the worst occurs and a firefighter is surrounded by a blaze. Wearing a fire shelter is like wearing a tent over yourself.

The great fire near Oakland, California, was different from the Yellowstone fire. It started in the hills and trails near the city, caused by lightning or, perhaps, by human carelessness. However, it menaced not only the hills, woods, and villages, but also the large city of Oakland.

As the inferno raged over the hills, it burned almost everything in its path. People wet their houses down in an effort to save them. In most cases, however, all that was left of the homes and other buildings after the conflagration had passed were blackened chimneys.

Brenda's grandparents lived in the hills near Oakland. They listened to reports of the fires getting closer and closer and wondered whether to evacuate or not. Finally, when the air around their house was filled with a blizzard of black ash, they knew it was time to leave. Everything smelled and tasted of fire. It was afternoon, but the sky was as dark as night.

Brenda and her family came in two cars and two pickup trucks to help her grandparents. They managed to save some of the furniture and smaller objects. They also took all of the most important papers and valuables.

Brenda's responsibility was to move Grandma and Grandpa's two parakeets, Woody and Schuyler. She covered their cage with a damp cover and put all their food and toys in a tote bag.

The family dog, Mittens, had disappeared. When they were ready to leave, he still had not returned. They stayed as long as they could, then sadly drove away from Grandma and Grandpa's house just as the roads were closed. People were being allowed to leave, but no one was permitted to enter the area.

Brenda shook as she clutched the parakeets' cage. Recalling Yellowstone, she feared for poor little Mittens. He had never been out alone in his spoiled, pampered life.

Schuyler and Woody were happy in their new home in Brenda's bedroom. They had their old, familiar cage, their well-used toys, and the attention of eight people, who played with them.

When the fires were out and people were permitted up in the hills again, Brenda went with her grandparents to the place where their old home stood. What a terrible scene it was! Everywhere you looked there were blackened ruins. Soot covered everything. All that was left of her grandparents' house were two chimneys and the stone steps. Suddenly something moved in the place where the hot tub had been. A filthy tan-and-white creature stirred.

"Mittens!" shrieked Grandma.

If only dogs could communicate. No one could understand how Mittens had survived the inferno, but he was almost untouched by the fire. Only his fluffy tail and the curly mane around his neck were badly singed.

You know dogs! Without his beautiful tail to wag and his neck fur, Mittens had lost all his confidence. He felt robbed of his dignity. Besides that, he had to suffer being dunked in the sink and given a bath to remove the black ash and smell of smoke.

 Underline the correct answer to each question.

1. Why do you think the rangers would not let Josh and Abner help?
   a. The rangers thought Josh and Abner may have started the fire.
   b. It was too serious a fire for untrained people.
   c. The boys did not have written notes signed by their parents.
   d. There were not enough hoses to go around.

2. Why was Brenda in Burton Woods?
   a. to study the habits of beavers   b. to climb high mountains
   c. to map out the trails   d. to study the habits of birds

3. There was a "blizzard" around the grandparents' home. What was it?
   a. an ice storm   b. a snow storm
   c. lightning and hail   d. blackened ashes

4. What is the main idea of the story?
   a. the life of a park ranger   b. how park rangers are trained
   c. the horrors of fires   d. how helicopters help in fires

5. What are firebreaks?
   a. certain rest periods that forest rangers receive
   b. breaks that forest rangers can suffer while fighting fires
   c. areas cleared of all dried wood that could burn
   d. breakdowns of firefighting equipment

6. Why did the lodgepole pine trees burn so easily?
   a. They have much juice or sap.
   b. These trees attract lightning more than other trees.
   c. They were dead and dry.
   d. The story did not say.

7. What made the fires in Oakland and Yellowstone spread so rapidly?

   a. little moisture and unusually high winds

   b. no rain and no breezes

   c. hot summer weather and too much bright sunlight

   d. the thousands of campfires that were not extinguished

8. Underline each object below that might be a firebreak in a forest fire.

   a. a lumberyard

   b. a large parking lot near a wide highway

   c. a lake or a river

   d. the ocean

   e. a chain saw

   f. land cleared down to the rocks

   g. junked cars

B **Write the correct word from the Word Box next to each meaning.**

─────── Word Box ───────		
pampered	evacuate	conscientious
simultaneous	dales	ignite
engulf	fire retardant	inferno
conflagration	glimpse	extinguish

1. at the same time _____

2. a huge blaze _____

3. honest, hard-working _____

4. spoiled, coddled _____Pampered_____

5. a quick look at _____

6. to put out _____

7. very slow to burn _____

8. to move out _____

9. to light _____

10. to surround _____

11. low places between hills _____

10

Here are some questions to make you think. Can you predict what will happen next? Look in the Prediction Box. Write the correct outcome under each story.

Prediction Box

a. They shovel dirt over the campfire.
b. The dead wood might be ignited by sparks.
c. Since rock and stone do not burn, the fire might go out.
d. The fire might attack and burn the firefighters.
e. They dig a fireproof cave.
f. The beetles would leave the lodgepole trees.
g. They might get bulldozers to help.

---

1. The firefighters dig down to the bare rock when digging a firebreak. What might happen next?

   _____ c _____

   _____

2. A fire is advancing rapidly. Digging with hand tools is not fast enough. What might the rangers do next?

   _____ a _____

   _____

3. The campers have finished eating. They are getting ready to leave the campsite. What might happen next?

   _____ f _____

   _____

4. Several hundred firefighters are struggling to extinguish a roaring blaze. The wind suddenly shifts in another direction! What could happen next?

   _____ D _____

   _____

5. Campers build their campfire next to the dead lodgepole pine trees. What might happen next?

   _____ B _____

   _____

Throughout history, in every part of the world, people have needed or wanted things that they did not make or grow or catch themselves. Long ago, when there was no such thing as money, the only way people could get these things was by trading, or *bartering.*

People bartered with one another for food, clothes, tools, ornaments, and furniture. Farmers got fish by swapping corn or wheat for them. Fishermen got furs from the hunters. The hunters got vegetables and grain from the farmers. The metal workers traded their tools for the hunters' meat.

Bartering worked very well as long as people lived simple lives. Then people needed more and more things. Trading to get just the thing they wanted could take a very long time. Sometimes, too, the Smiths, Joneses, Hunters, and Fishers could not agree on how much one large fish, a beautiful bearskin, some lovely feathers, or some colorful shells and beads were worth.

The Farmers also had trouble dragging heavy sacks of onions over to the Smiths to trade for a new metal knife or a stone axe. Mrs. Diggs had to balance a heavy basket on her head to swap the salt she dug up for the garment Mr. Tailor put together from the cloth he had received from Mrs. Weaver.

Then someone got a good idea. Instead of everyone trading different things, perhaps people could agree on one common thing that could be used to pay for other things. There had to be something that almost everyone would accept, something that was special enough that people would take it in payment for their goods or their work.

People tried many different items, but there were things that not everyone had a use for, such as Mr. Wright's wheels or Mrs. Herd's goats. Finally, they decided on small pieces of metal made of copper, bronze, iron, brass, tin, lead, silver, or gold.

These small pieces of metal were the world's first money. Here are some of the characteristics that made these metal pieces an easier way to pay for goods and work:

1. They were durable.
2. They were *portable,* or easy to carry.
3. They were convenient to use.
4. They were only used to pay for things or work.
5. There were enough, but not too many of them.

At first, these metal pieces were easily divisible into smaller pieces. They were made in all different sizes and shapes, such as rings, bars, knives, hoes, and dolphins. As time went on, country after country made its own special coins to be used as money.

The Greeks were the first people to use coins. By 700 B.C., they were pressing designs on their coins to identify the city-states from which they came. This practice still goes on today. All countries have different designs on their coins, so people can readily see where the money is issued.

Sometimes dishonest people shaved the metal off the edges of the coins, melted down the metal, and made new coins. One of the last changes made in coins was to put a special edging around each coin. This made it possible for the person receiving the money to tell at once whether someone had tampered with the rim of a coin.

A   **Underline the correct answer to each question.**

1. Why were coins printed with different designs?
   a. to show the artists who made the designs
   b. to show pictures of Greek gods and goddesses
   c. to show how much silver was in each coin
   d. to show where the coins originated

2. Why do you think people began to use paper money?
   a. They ran out of new designs for the coins.
   b. Presidents of the United States wanted their pictures on paper money.
   c. All around the world, metals became scarce.
   d. A large amount of coins was too heavy to carry.

3. Why must coins be durable?
   a. They have to last for thousands of years.
   b. They have to be handled by many people.
   c. They have to be divided into smaller amounts.
   d. They have to be easy to carry.

4. What did people do before they used metal pieces for payment?
   a. They traded one thing for others.
   b. They stamped coins.
   c. They used paper money.
   d. They had to produce everything they needed.

5. Why do you think all coins are not made of gold?
   a. Gold is too common.
   b. Gold is too easy to find.
   c. Gold is too rare.
   d. Gold is too hard to make into coins.

6. Which of these things would <u>not</u> have been good to use to buy things?
   a. shells   b. silver
   c. oak leaves   d. cattle

7. What would be a good title for this selection?
   a. Bartering for Food and Clothing
   b. The Development of Coins
   c. The Different Greek Coins
   d. The Use of Paper Money

Deposit these coins in the bank by writing the correct word next to each meaning.

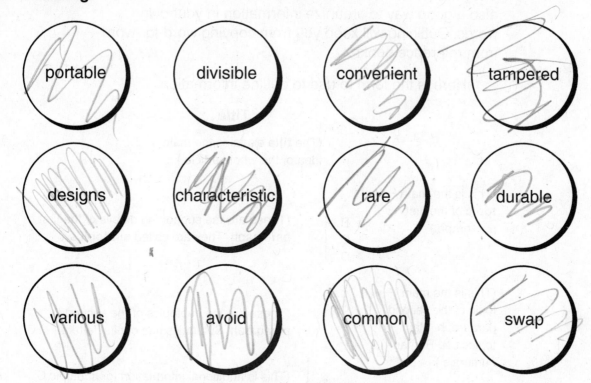

portable | divisible | convenient | tampered
designs | characteristic | rare | durable
various | avoid | common | swap

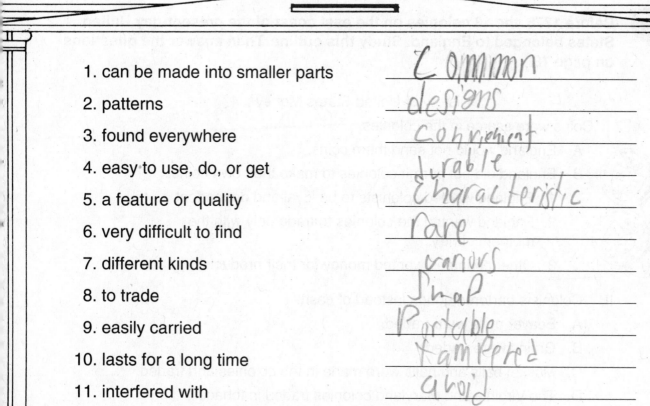

1. can be made into smaller parts — _Common_

2. patterns — _designs_

3. found everywhere — _convenient_

4. easy to use, do, or get — _durable_

5. a feature or quality — _Characteristic_

6. very difficult to find — _rare_

7. different kinds — _various_

8. to trade — _Swap_

9. easily carried — _Portable_

10. lasts for a long time — _tampered_

11. interfered with — _avoid_

Outlines are a way to make information more compact. They make information easier to remember. Outlines are also a good way to organize information in your own words. Outlining will keep you from copying word-for-word from reference books.

Here is the form to use to outline information.

Title

(The **title** explains the main idea of the whole article.)

(This is the **main topic** of the first paragraph.) → I.
  A.
  B.   (These are the supporting details of the first
  C.   paragraph. They are called **subtopics**.)
  D.

(This is the main topic of the second paragraph. Main topics use Roman numerals.) → II.
  A.
  B.   (These are the subtopics of the second
  C.   paragraph. Subtopics use capital letters.)
    1.
    2.   (This is additional information for subtopic C.
    3.   These use Arabic numbers.)

C **Before 1776, the 13 colonies on the east coast of the present-day United States belonged to England. Study this outline. Then answer the questions on page 18.**

History of United States Money

I. Coins were scarce in the colonies.

  A. England would not send them coins.
  B. England did not permit colonies to make their own coins.
    1. England wanted colonists to be loyal and dependent.
    2. England wanted the colonies to trade only with the mother country.
    3. Other countries wanted money for their products.

II. Colonists bartered goods instead of cash.
  A. Beaver pelts were traded.
  B. Grains were traded.
  C. Musket balls and nails were made in the colonies and traded.
  D. The Virginia and Maryland colonies traded in tobacco.
  E. Indian wampum beads made from shells were accepted as money by other colonies and Indians.

III. Coins from other countries were left in the colonies by sailors whose ships came there.
   A. English shillings
   B. French coins
   C. Dutch coins
   D. Spanish coins called "pieces of eight"
      1. Spanish coins could be chopped into 8 pie-shaped pieces.
      2. These pieces, called "bits," were used for smaller change.

IV. In 1652, the Massachusetts Colony started making coins.
   A. The coins were silver.
      1. Pine tree shillings were worth 3 pennies.
      2. Oak tree shillings were worth 6 pennies.
      3. Designs were stamped on the coins.
   B. Massachusetts was breaking English law by making coins.
   C. Only the English kings could issue coins.
   D. From then until 1776, all Massachusetts coins were dated 1652.
      1. In 1652, England had no king to issue coins.
      2. No law was broken by Massachusetts.

V. Massachusetts was the first colony to produce paper money.
   A. In 1690, it issued notes called *Bills of Credit*.
   B. These notes financed the first French and Indian War.
      1. This was a war between the French and English colonies.
      2. It was fought for the control of eastern North America.

VI. By 1775, the colonies were ready to rebel against England.
   A. Each colony issued its own paper money to pay for the Revolutionary War.
   B. The Continental Congress issued its own paper money.

1. How many main topics are in this outline? _____6_____

2. What is the title of this outline?

   _____history of united States money_____

3. What is some additional information found in main topic IV, subtopic D?

   a. Massachusetts printed paper money.

   b. There was no English king in 1652.

   c. England did not send coins to the colonies.

   d. The French and Indian War was fought.

4. How many subtopics are found in main topic I? _____3_____

5. What did you learn from main topic II, subtopic C?

   _____musket balls and nails were made in the colonies and traded_____

6. What is the main idea of main topic II?

   a. how Spanish coins were cut

   b. how the colonists got Dutch coins

   c. why England wanted the colonies to be dependent

   d. what the early colonists traded

7. What is the purpose of this outline?

   a. to organize facts about United States money

   b. to organize facts about English trade with the colonies

   c. to tell the history of the French and Indian War

   d. to make people collect coins

8. How many supporting details are found in main topic V, subtopic B?

   _____

9. What were some of the first coins issued by Massachusetts?

   a. pieces of eight   b. maple leaf pennies

   c. pine tree notes of credit   d. pine tree shillings

10. All the colonies began to print paper money when the war started. What war was it?

    a. The War of 1812   b. The Civil War

    c. The Revolutionary War   d. The French and Indian War

D **Read the following article. Then shorten the information by outlining it. Some parts of the outline have been done for you. Use the Topic and Subtopic Box and the Additional Information Box to help you complete the outline. Skim the paragraphs if you need help.**

A Major Pest

What can give you an almost unbearable itch? What makes normal human beings scratch at their skins wildly? It's the tiny but nasty mosquito, a major pest. Here is some information that will help you recognize and avoid these villains.

The mosquito's head has large, bulging eyes which can detect even slight movements in the world about it. They help the mosquito to capture its prey. Two bushy antennae on the head smell and sense anything in the mosquito's world. Mosquitoes' mouths are adapted for eating the nectar from flowers. Female mosquitoes' mouths have long sucking tubes which enable them to bite and to suck the blood of their victims. The males' mouths have no sucking tube, and they cannot bite.

Under the head is the *thorax*, which has two thin, almost-transparent wings. The wings enable this pest to fly forward, backward, and sideways at speeds up to thirty miles an hour. Also on the thorax are six long, very slender legs. The mosquito's legs are very distinctive because they are as long or longer than the insect's entire body. The legs are what we humans see most clearly.

There are 3,000 types of mosquitoes, and they are found all over the world, except in oceans and deserts. Mosquitoes are very difficult to get rid of because they lay their eggs in any tiny pool of stagnant water. The eggs are laid in quiet ponds, old tires, bird baths, tin cans, pails, gutters, wet leaves, hollows in trees, flower pots, rain puddles, and even in vases inside your home.

It's certainly lucky for humans that fish, birds, frogs, toads, and other insects enjoy feasting on mosquitoes. Otherwise we would all see and feel thousands of the pests constantly.

Mosquitoes can be very dangerous to the health of human beings and animals, especially in hot, tropical climates. They carry serious diseases such as yellow fever, malaria, and encephalitis. A sickness called *dengue fever,* which is carried by mosquitoes, is spreading through many warm islands. Heartworm in dogs is another disease caused by these pesky insects.

Topic and Subtopic Box	Additional Information Box
Has two wings	Used by females to bite and to suck blood
Two bushy antennae	Ponds
Where mosquitoes are found	Encephalitis
Is under the head	Can detect any slight movement
Causes dangerous diseases	Adapted so males unable to bite or to suck blood
Has six legs	Aid in capturing prey
	Old tires
	Adapted so males and females can eat nectar
	Tree hollows
	Are transparent

The Mosquito

I. The head

   A. Large, bulging eyes

     1. _Can detect any slight movement_

     2. _aid in capturing prey_

   B. _____

   C. Mouth

     1. _____

     2. _____

     3. _____

II. The thorax

  A. _____

  B. _____

    1. _____

    2. Help mosquito fly

  C. _____

    1. Long and slender

    2. As long or longer than the entire body

    3. Clearly seen

III. _____

  A. Almost all over the world

    1. Not in deserts

    2. Not in oceans

  B. Eggs laid in stagnant water

    1. _____

    2. _____

    3. Rain puddles

    4. Tin cans

    5. _____

    6. Flower vases

IV. _____

  A. In humans

    1. Malaria

    2. Yellow fever

    3. _____

    4. Dengue fever

  B. Heartworm in dogs

In 1792, Congress made new coins and a new currency system for the new country, the United States. However, there were still so many foreign coins being used in these former colonies that in 1793 the government declared foreign coins legal and part of the United States currency system. This circle graph shows the percentage of each foreign coin still in use in 1800. Study the information and answer the questions.

Foreign Coins Being Used in the United States in 1800

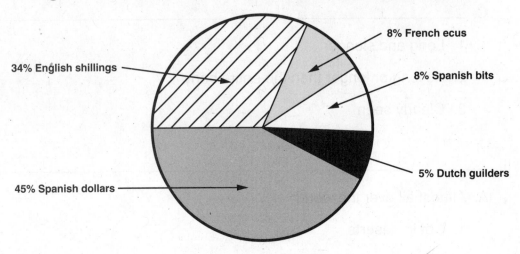

1. Which foreign coins were being used the most?

   Spanish dollars

2. Which two groups of coins were the same in number?

   French ecus   Spanish bits

3. Of which coins were there the fewest?

   dutch guilders

4. What is the difference between the percent of English shillings and the percent of Spanish dollars?

   _11_

5. French ecus were what percent of the total of foreign coins? _8%_

6. What two groups of coins made up 50% of the total number of foreign coins being used?

   Spanish dollars and dutch guilders

7. What does this graph show?

   Foreign coins blend used in the United States in 1800

8. What percentage of Italian lira were being used?

   a. 40%   b. 6%   c. The graph does not show this.

Thursday & Friday

We're back! The detective team of Donna and Nicky is here to solve another mystery. Our latest case involved our father's friend, Lester Judd. We went to visit him recently and he told us this puzzling tale.

A few months ago in England, an unexpected discovery had been made. In cleaning out the attic of an ancient house, someone had found a secret closet in the wall. About a hundred early photographs were found in it. They had been taken and dated in 1860 and 1861 by a man named Archer. Dad said that Mr. Archer had been an important person in the early history of photography. People had written about him in books, encyclopedias, and newspapers.

Experts had examined the paper, the chemicals, and the kinds of negatives used. As far as they could tell, everything was what the early photographers had used in the 1860s. Because Archer's photographs were so rare, many collectors wanted them. Mr. Judd had the chance to buy a few of them for $60,000.

I almost fell out of my chair. Dad's hobby was taking pictures. Could it be that a hundred years from now, Dad's photos could be worth that much?

"This is very exciting, Lester. I can hardly wait to set eyes upon these antiques," Dad said to Mr. Judd.

"They're all studies of young street waifs," said Mrs. Judd.

"What are waifs?" interrupted Nicky.

Mr. Judd explained. Back in the late 1800s in London, many poor children lived alone in the streets. They were called waifs. They had no parents and no one to care for them. They slept in alleys and empty buildings. For food, they either stole, begged, or starved. Sometimes they earned a few pennies doing hard work.

Nicky and I could not really believe that children could be treated so wickedly. When Mrs. Judd took out a folder of faded photos, we joined Dad in looking at them.

"Ohh!" we exclaimed as we studied the pictures of ragged, mistreated waifs.

Two pictures of the same little girl interested me. She was beautiful, with huge, light eyes. In one picture, I saw her back as she struggled with a heavy wheelbarrow. Her hair was a mop of dirty tangles hanging almost to her waist. Nicky was more interested in a photo of a skinny boy holding a torn coat around him. Both children looked starved and sad.

"The experts are right," said Dad. "The materials seem to be the correct ones for 1860. I've seen some of Archer's photos in a museum. They had the same sort of brownish coloring."

Mr. Judd said, "But none of the experts will state positively that these are real Archer photographs and not forgeries. I would like to buy them, but I'm afraid."

Then the Judds started to talk about another expert from Washington, D.C., who was going to arrive on Monday to test the old pictures.

"If they're not forgeries, I wish I had enough money to buy one," Dad said. "I would love to have it in my collection."

Nicky could not stop examining the photos of waifs. We were not allowed to handle the pictures, but Mrs. Judd spread them out so that we could see them better. I only looked again to see what Nicky was staring at for so long.

Finally Nicky spoke. "I don't know what it is, but there's something wrong with the wrinkles in the kids' clothes."

"Oh, come on, Nick. What can you know about 1860?" I replied.

Then I suddenly realized that I wasn't doing what I always told everyone else to do. To be a detective, you must look and listen carefully and then think. I started to listen carefully to my brother.

"What do you mean?" I asked, bending over the pictures once more.

Nicky pointed to the beautiful little girl. "Look at those messy, ragged clothes. But in with all the wrinkles, under her hair, I can just make out two straight lines."

I could hardly tell what he was looking at. "Do you have a magnifying glass?" I asked Mrs. Judd.

She laughed, but she handed us one.

"It's on the boy, too," Nicky whispered to me. "It is strange."

We peered through the magnifying glass. I got excited. Nicky was right. I saw something else that seemed out of place. I said nothing aloud, because I didn't want the Judds to laugh at us. Dad might be embarrassed.

Nicky and I needed to check some of the odd things we had noticed on the pictures. We looked in the last volume of the Judds' encyclopedia. Some of what we were looking for was not in the encyclopedia. We were lucky, though. We found enough information by using the index in another book.

Nicky and I decided we would tell Dad what we had discovered. Then he could tell the Judds. We were afraid they would think we were silly. But our plan, as usual, did not work exactly right.

Mrs. Judd came in and inquired, "Are you ready to report your expert findings yet?" She looked at us. The expression on her face seemed to say, "Let's be patient with these kids playing detective."

I said, "Yes, but we may be wrong, because it's hard to see much on those dirty, creased clothes. There is something unusual here. Nicky noticed that usually the wrinkles go in all directions, but there are also little lines that go only straight up and down. On the back of the pretty little girl, almost hidden by her long, filthy hair, we saw the same straight lines. With the magnifying glass, we figured out that she has a long zipper down the back of her dress. See it there." I pointed.

"Most of the shots of her show the front only, so it is hard to notice. Once we knew what to look for, we found that all the boy waifs have zippers on their clothes, too. Only tiny parts of them can be seen." I stopped.

Then Nicky started, "Zippers weren't invented until 1893. They were first used on clothes in 1931. Kids in 1860 could not have had zippers. The photos have to be forgeries. Donna noticed something, too. See the skinny little waif who looks as if he is starving?"

I reported on my find. "The clawlike hands holding the ragged coat around the waif's bony chest hardly show. With the magnifying glass, though, you can just see the end of one of those sticky bandages you put on cuts and scrapes. In one of Mr. Judd's books, we read that they weren't invented until the 1940s."

"Someone dishonest is playing a trick on old photo collectors!" exclaimed Dad.

What compliments were showered on us! Mr. and Mrs. Judd piled praise on Nicky and me until even our proud father turned red with embarrassment.

Mr. Judd joked, "I could have lost a lot of money. Instead of paying an expert to fly in from Washington, I should have asked Donna and Nicky for help. I am very grateful to you."

A **Underline the correct answer for each question.**

1. What did Mr. Judd want to buy?

    a. some beautiful photographs from George Washington's time

    b. some of the first photographs ever taken

    c. some pictures showing how children are being mistreated in England

    d. some new cameras that could take pictures faster, clearer, and better than the ones we now have

2. Experts had studied the pictures. What are **experts**?

    a. people who have been successful photographers

    b. people who know a little about many subjects

    c. people whose main work is finding forgeries

    d. people who know a lot about a subject

3. According to Mr. Judd's story, in 1861

    a. photography was in its most popular period.

    b. the art of photography was in its early stages.

    c. photography was invented.

    d. photographers used the same materials and equipment as they do today.

4. Why was Mr. Judd worried about buying the photographs?

    a. He did not have enough money to get the expensive photos.

    b. The photos were the wrong color and too faded to be Archer's photographs.

    c. The paper the pictures were printed on was not the kind used in 1860.

    d. He was not certain the pictures had really been taken by Archer in 1860.

5. What did Donna and Nicky discover about the photographs?

    a. They were forgeries.

    b. They were too wrinkled.

    c. They were too faded.

    d. They had Archer's signature hidden in creases on the clothing.

6. What had Nicky noticed that seemed strange to him?

    a. not enough wrinkles

    b. too many creases

    c. perfectly straight wrinkles

    d. The children on the photos wore nice clothes.

7. What important clues helped Donna and Nicky solve this case?

   a. seeing the wrong kind of zippers on the clothing

   b. seeing that the zippers were in the wrong places

   c. seeing the clothing fastened by sticky bandages for cuts

   d. seeing things on the pictures that had not yet been invented in 1860

8. The two young detectives were not sure what the clues meant. How did they check their information?

   a. by asking experts

   b. by calling the library

   c. by researching

   d. by guessing

9. What is the main idea of this story?

   a. Reading an encyclopedia can change a child into a photography expert.

   b. Examine everything carefully before buying.

   c. Photography is a popular hobby.

   d. An old photograph is valuable.

10. The photographs were supposed to be of

   a. lovely English gardens.

   b. poor, homeless children.

   c. ancient homes and clothes.

   d. secret closets in attics.

B On each line are two words that are antonyms, or opposite in meaning. Circle the antonyms.

1. towards	across	beneath	away from
2. pouring	difficult	simple	flooded
3. creased	repaired	broke	exchanged
4. strange	odd	arrive	familiar
5. earth	early	late	invisible
6. behind	farther	upon	closer
7. supply	tumble	mumble	shout
8. piled on	unloaded	unwashed	hugged
9. huge	filthy	starved	spotless
10. ordered	inquired	invented	replied
11. completed	struggled	started	commanded

C **Choose a word from below to complete each sentence. Some words may be used twice.**

forgeries   positively   rare
photography   peer   miserable
compliment   filthy   report
mistreat   struggled   realized
magnify   creases   antique

1. To make something larger to see it more clearly is to _____ magnify _____

2. Someone who is very unhappy, upset, or ill is _____ struggled _____.

3. False copies that are claimed to be the real thing are _____ forgeries _____.

4. Another word for *surely* or *certainly* is _____ positively _____.

5. Something that is very unclean is _____ filthy _____.

6. To tell about an event is to _____ report _____ it.

7. The act of taking pictures with a camera is called _____ Photog _____

8. To treat badly is to _____.

9. A _____ Antique _____ is a form of praise.

10. An object used long ago is known as an _____.

11. Wrinkles are also called _____ rare creas _____.

12. Something that is seldom seen or not common is _____ rare _____.

13. To examine something closely, you _____ at it.

14. The photograph will be easier to see if we _____ it.

15. The teacher asked us to make an oral _____.

A time line is a good way to put events in the correct order. It can also be used to organize some kinds of materials into a shorter, more easily readable form. To fill out a time line, you must understand dates. Start with the earliest date at the left of the line and continue adding dates in order until the latest date is at the right end of the line. Place these dates in the correct places on the time line. Then complete the time chart on page 31 by placing the events and their dates in correct order.

The History of Cameras

1720—The idea of using film to take pictures started.

1568—A lens was placed on the hole in a box for a clearer view. The picture was reversed.

1830—Daguerre learned how to take a picture that lasted. It took an hour to make the photograph.

1850—Archer invented a better way to make negatives.

1822—Photographs were printed on a glass plate. It took eight hours to make the picture.

1569—A mirror was placed behind the lens in the box so pictures would not be reversed.

1841—Talbot invented the negative so that pictures could be copied over and over.

Time Line

Time Chart

Date	Event
1553	A box with a hole in it was made to focus a picture for artists.

 When looking up information, you usually find many facts about a subject. Some are relevant for what you need. Some are not relevant. **Relevant** means **important for your purposes**.

Read the problem below. Put an **X** by each fact that is not relevant.

Elizabeth Drake was the daughter of wealthy parents. In 1878, she read about the homeless waifs in a large English city. Elizabeth decided to start a soup kitchen, a place where children could be fed a free meal each day.

1. Elizabeth's grandmother gave her a large sum of money to buy meat, fish, and potatoes.
2. Many waifs could be found in the alleys around the harbor.
3. A merchant offered some land he owned near the harbor to use as a small park for the children of Elizabeth's friends and their nursemaids.
4. Elizabeth's parents gave her a trip to France for her eighteenth birthday.
5. Elizabeth's uncle let her live with him free of charge.
6. There was an empty store on a street facing the harbor that could be used as a soup kitchen.
7. Some of Elizabeth's cousins offered to spend one day a week helping at the soup kitchen.
8. Grocers gave free stale bread and leftover vegetables to use in the soup.

"Why did I ever think that a jungle trip would be fun?" exclaimed Amanda Yamamota as she slapped at a huge insect stinging her nose.

Her brother, Larry, squashed a hairy spider feasting on his ear. He cried out, "We thought exploring a rain forest would be exciting, not deadly."

Their friend, Rosa Garcia, agreed. She said, "Remember how we begged our parents to take us along? How could we have known that this jungle would be so thick that we would have to chop our way through it?"

"I'd give anything for a path for my tired feet," said Larry. "These bushes and vines wear me out!"

Jimmy Garcia said, "The temperature is about 100° now. And the humidity is very high, too. Living near the equator is not comfortable."

Jimmy, Amanda, Rosa, and Larry were the only youngsters with a group of scientists searching the jungle. They were looking for some special plants. These rare plants had flowers not found anywhere else in the world. The few blossoms brought back from this rain forest had had a beautiful fragrance. Perfume made from the petals was the most popular ever sold. Besides that, testing showed that the flower stems held a liquid. This liquid could be used to make a medicine that cured serious illness. The flowers had been named Mysterias. Explorers were combing jungles everywhere to find more of them.

Perfume makers and drug companies had hired the children's parents to explore parts of the South American rain forest. They hoped to discover a large number of the Mysterias there. Bringing them back to the United States would help many people.

The two families had joined a group of 33 people and 20 burros. They had started their journey on February 1 into a warm, steamy, unknown world. The rain forest was filled with noisy, brightly colored birds and bugs. Because the jungle was so near the equator, its climate was hot all year long. The daily rains and the heat made all the plants grow quickly.

At the end of each month, two people and a burro were sent back to the United States. Each time they reported their failure to find any Mysterias. It was now July 23 and almost time to send another sad report.

The whole party had stopped to take a cooling swim in a clear pool. Because Jimmy was itching from several insect bites, he took out a bar of soap. He was washing himself when he felt a movement close to him.

A young, small crocodile, its jaws wide open, wanted a taste of Jimmy's right leg.

"Help!" screeched Jimmy, scrambling out of the water. "Crocodile! Crocodile!"

In seconds, all the people were up on land. The hungry crocodile was left with only a bar of soap. But as the people watched, he swallowed it! The last time the group saw him, he was paddling away in a cloud of bubbles!

As Amanda sat on the side of the pool, watching the bubbly crocodile swim away, she saw a log on the bank. "I'll grab that to pull myself up!" the girl thought.

Both of her arms were outstretched, and her fingers almost touched the greenish-brown log. Suddenly, the log whipped around. Amanda screamed as she found herself face-to-face with an even larger crocodile.

Fear gave Amanda's feet wings. She never knew how she did it, but she dodged to the side. Amanda expected at any second to feel the crocodile's teeth on her legs, pulling her down into the water. That was what the huge creatures sometimes did with their victims.

Amanda's strong leap carried her quite a distance on land. Then her foot caught on a tangled vine. Headfirst she fell into thick underbrush. Amanda lay there stunned for some time. Finally, she opened her eyes to an odd sight.

Some beautiful, pale yellow flowers grew among the bushes. Hundreds of insects flew around the flowers. The insects circled the blossoms and then landed on them.

"These flowers really attract all kinds of insects," thought Amanda.

As she watched, suddenly the petals of the flowers snapped shut. Many bugs were trapped inside. All that could be seen of the flowers now were tight, slender yellow buds.

"I do believe that these flowers eat insects," thought Amanda.

The scientists decided to remain there to observe what would happen next. They took many photographs of the plant.

For a week, the buds stayed shut. Then one day the routine was repeated. A curious, baby monkey heard noises and swung near the flowers. The lovely, yellow petals opened.

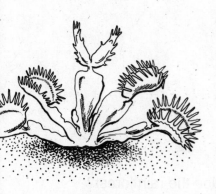

Then, one blossom grabbed the little monkey's tail and a tug of war followed. With all of its strength, the baby monkey pulled and pulled! But it was unsuccessful. Then the flower snipped off a tiny part of the creature's tail. The monkey dashed up the nearest tree screeching.

"It's a meat-eating flower!" exclaimed Dr. Ruth Yamamota. "As usual, this plant will be named after its discoverer. We'll call it the Amandamum."

At once, the scientists made plans to dig up several of the plants. With the soil, the plants would be sent back to the United States. Two members of the science group and a burro headed back with good news for the first time.

Dr. Garcia said, "I hope we can raise these flowers safely in our country. We will be able to kill pests such as gypsy moths, fruit flies, locusts, and other harmful insects. Farmers can put this blossom to good use! We will have to make sure it does not destroy helpful insects and small animals, however."

Dr. Ian Smith added, "Though we've made an important discovery, we still haven't found the Mysteria. We should keep on searching."

(to be continued)

Underline the correct answer to each question.

1. Why did the scientists go to the rain forest?

    a. to count the raindrops

    b. to find a meat-eating plant

    c. to find special flowers

    d. to find out more about monkeys

2. What kind of story is this?

    a. a description of rain forests

    b. a fictional adventure tale

    c. a science story about jungle animals

    d. a scientific study of American plants

3. From what you have read here, how would you describe the rain forest?

    a. warm and shady   b. dry and hot

    c. like a desert   d. damp and hot

4. What did the young crocodile want to do?

    a. eat Jimmy   b. eat a bar of soap

    c. swim with people   d. blow bubbles

5. Which of these would not be found in this rain forest?

    a. large trees and bushes   b. brightly colored birds

    c. beautiful flowers   d. a wide, twisting road

B **Details in a story tell where, when, why, how, who, and what about the topic and/or the action. Skim the story to find these details or facts. Write the key words that help you locate the information and then answer the questions. One is done for you.**

1. Who were the four youngsters? **youngsters—Jimmy, Amanda,**

   Rosa, and Larry

2. What color were the flowers of the meat-eating plant? _____

   _____

3. What two characters had a tug-of-war? _____

   _____

4. What did Larry squash?_____

5. What did the small crocodile want? _____

6. What might the large crocodile have done to Amanda? _____

   _____

C **Where does this story take place? Where is the rain forest? Skim the story and look at the map. Then answer the following questions.**

1. On what continent is the rain forest located? _____

2. The rain forest is located close to the _____.

3. From which country had the explorers come? _____

4. On which continent is this country located? _____

5. In which direction did the explorers travel to reach the rain forest?

   _____

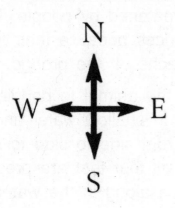

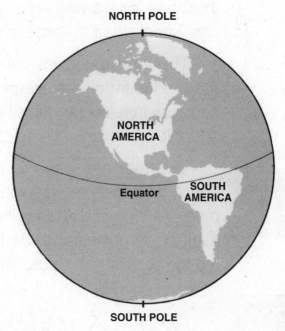

D **Answer these questions by looking at the map or skimming the story. Underline the correct answer or fill in the blank for each question.**

1. Places closer to the equator are (colder, hotter).

2. As we move away from the equator, the weather usually becomes (cooler, warmer).

3. The lower the temperature, the (colder, hotter) it is.

4. The higher the temperature, the (cooler, warmer) it is.

5. The North Pole and the South Pole are as far away as possible from the equator. The South Pole has (cool, very cold, warm, very hot) weather all year long.

6. Rain forests are (near, far from) the equator.

7. Rain forests are always (cold, hot) and always have (high, low) temperatures.

8. In which direction will the explorers travel to take the Mysterias home?

   _____

 37

Crocodiles

Crocodiles, like other reptiles, have tough, scaly skin that protects them from enemies. Even their stomachs are covered with hard scales. Crocodiles have long, powerful tails that they can swing around quickly. One slap from this tail can knock over a large animal.

Though crocodiles can live well on land and in the water, they hide under the water when threatened by people. They can run fast on land for short distances because their four short legs lift up, raising their stomachs off the ground.

The feet are webbed to enable the animal to paddle about and to help keep its balance in shallow water and mud. The crocodile wiggles its tail from side to side to steer itself when swimming. At that time, all four feet are pressed tightly against its sides, and it zooms along in the water.

The crocodile's nostrils are on top of its nose in the front of its long head. Air is inhaled through the nostrils. Its eyes are set farther back on the head to fool the prey. Sometimes the eyes and the nostrils are kept elevated above the water line with the rest of the head below. In this way, the crocodile lies unnoticed by other animals coming for a drink of water. Crocodiles have even been known to jump up out of the water to capture birds flying low.

Because a crocodile resting in the water is disguised as a log, it even catches unaware large animals coming to drink. The crocodile with one swipe of its powerful tail can stun the large beast. Then the reptile grabs the animal and kills it.

For swimming underwater, the crocodile's muscles close off its nose and ears to keep water out. Clear eyelids like transparent curtains slide across the eyes to protect them from water. A flap of skin at the back of the mouth shuts and keeps water out of the throat. The crocodile stays completely underwater for long periods of time.

Crocodiles have 60 to 80 teeth. When a tooth breaks or wears out, a new one grows. These teeth can grab, bite, and tear meat into smaller pieces. They cannot do what your teeth do—chew! Crocodiles swallow their food in large hunks.

_____ 1. Crocodiles seldom walk on rocky land. Because of their short legs, their stomachs get scraped on the stones.

_____ 2. A crocodile's body is tough and scaly.

_____ 3. Underwater, eyelids cover a crocodile's eyes and keep it from seeing.

_____ 4. When chasing a fast fish, the crocodile moves its legs quickly in the water.

_____ 5. Crocodiles catch animals sometimes by striking them down with their strong tails.

_____ 6. The only use for the crocodile's tail is as a weapon.

_____ 7. The front teeth of crocodiles perform the task of chewing.

_____ 8. Loss of too many teeth has caused crocodiles to starve.

_____ 9. Crocodiles have been known to leap up to catch a flying bird.

_____ 10. The webbed feet of crocodiles help them swim faster.

_____ 11. Crocodiles can move rapidly on land but only for short distances.

_____ 12. Webbed feet enable the crocodile to balance itself in a swamp.

F **Choose a word from below to complete each sentence.**

```
──────────────── Word Box ────────────────
  journey      jungle      squash       routine
  success      vine        burro        attract
  equator      observed    strength     screech
  fragrance    liquid      temperature  humidity
```

1. The heat or coldness of something is its _____.

2. A sweet smell is a _____.

3. A loud cry is a _____.

4. Something watched carefully is _____.

5. The dampness of the air is called _____.

6. A long trip is a _____.

7. Something done well is a _____.

8. A climbing plant is a _____.

9. Something that pours is a _____.

10. To make something come close is to _____.

11. A kind of donkey is a _____.

12. An overgrown rain forest is a _____.

13. To smash flat is to _____.

14. To do something regularly is a _____.

15. The power in your muscles is called _____.

16. Flowers give off a _____.

17. One kind of vegetable is a _____.

40

Bright red and brilliant yellow flashed through the jungle as a bird flew from tree to vine. Amanda and Rosa had been waiting for this. Click went their cameras! Their job was to study that kind of bird. The explorers had discovered a pair of the colorful, unknown birds. The girls were photographing them. These birds were shaped like the North American cardinal, but their colors were much brighter.

Jimmy and Larry had a more demanding job. They were observing a black and purple bird that blended into the shadows. It could scarcely be seen. Larry was creeping to a thick tree trunk to get a better look at the bird's nest hidden in a hole in the trunk. Larry crawled closer and closer. Finally, he held onto the tree, trying to climb up. He raised one hand to a branch to pull himself nearer. At that moment, Rosa glanced his way, and she froze with fright.

"Don't move, Larry!" she called. "Stand still!"

Jimmy and Amanda also stopped to stare at her. Their long months in the jungle had taught them not to move in times of danger.

At first, Rosa was the only one to notice a movement. Then Larry felt the branch he was holding stir. Twisted around the branch, its green colors blending with the leaves, was a large, thick snake! When Larry grabbed the branch, he touched the snake at the same time.

"Quiet!" whispered Jimmy. "It's a boa!"

The reptile was as surprised as Larry! With a rapid movement it slithered from the tree and wrapped itself around the young explorer.

The group knew how to stand still to give the snake a chance to escape.

Jimmy said slowly, "I will go for help." Step by step he inched backward. He did not know that behind him, hidden in the tall grass, was a pit. Into the pit Jimmy stepped—down, down, down! As Jimmy crashed through the vines with a loud shriek, the noise frightened the birds. They squawked and screeched as they flew away. The disturbed boa twisted itself more tightly around Larry's body.

The two girls were very frightened. Jimmy had disappeared in the pit, and Larry was in danger of being squeezed to death. But their jungle training had taught them to think quickly. Rosa stayed by Larry, begging him not to move a muscle. She spoke in a slow whisper. Amanda knew she had to go for help. She did not make the same mistake that Jimmy did. She moved forward, noiselessly watching every step. She knew Larry's life might depend on her silence. She hurried to the tents where an adult was always on guard.

Amanda's calmness left her as soon as she saw the grownups. Tears poured down her cheeks. "Quick! Hurry!" she said. "Larry is being squeezed by a boa! Jimmy fell into a pit!"

The emergency team rushed into action. One woman remained to stand guard at the camp in case another of the work teams met some difficulty. All the others took their first-aid kits, ropes, and tools and started back with Amanda.

Their stay in the jungle had taught them to move quietly but rapidly. When Amanda made a signal to show they were near Larry, everyone became silent. The young girl, calm again, led them along quietly.

Soon they stood silently staring at Rosa and Larry. Two men tiptoed about, feeling with sticks. They were trying to locate the pit.

Larry, scarcely breathing, stood like a stone as the boa curled around his shoulders. Rosa watched. She was motionless, too. The seconds went by like hours. Would the boa crush the boy? Finally, seeing no danger, the snake slithered down and rustled away into the vines.

Amanda tried to joke. She said to her brother, "That boa loved you! It was hugging you for a long time."

As soon as Larry was free, the whole party rushed to the pit. They could hardly find it in the thick underbrush. The hole went down so far the bottom could not be seen. There was no sign of Jimmy. The explorers knew the boy could be in great danger.

Dr. Stewart was lowered on a long rope. He was gone some time before three sharp tugs showed he wanted to be raised.

"At the bottom, there's a fast, underground river that comes out of the ground on some rocks," he reported. "Jimmy must be in the water somewhere! We must find those rocks and follow the river!"

(to be continued)

A **Underline the correct answer to each question.**

1. Why did Jimmy fall into the pit?
   a. He was not watching where he was going.
   b. He was trying to see what was in the pit.
   c. He was following the boa.
   d. He wanted to photograph a bird's nest.

2. Why didn't Larry know the snake was on the branch?
   a. The snake was hidden in the hollow.
   b. The snake was hidden in the pit.
   c. The brilliant colors of the birds were shining in his eyes.
   d. The colors of the snake blended with the colors of the tree.

3. Which of these happened first?
   a. Larry tried to look in the hollow.
   b. The girls photographed the unknown birds.
   c. Jimmy walked backwards.
   d. Larry touched the boa.

4. Where was the bird's nest hidden?
   a. on a branch   b. in a hole in a tree
   c. in a hole in the ground   d. under a flowering vine

5. Which would be the best title for this story?

    a. Jimmy Explores the Pit

    b. Photographing Birds

    c. The Bite of the Boa

    d. Two Accidents

6. Which happened last in the story?

    a. Amanda brought back help.

    b. The boa twisted around Larry.

    c. Jimmy disappeared.

    d. Dr. Stewart gave the rope three tugs.

7. Some jungle birds have brilliant coloring. What does *brilliant* mean?

    a. bright   b. red

    c. dull   d. dark

8. Why was Larry climbing the tree?

    a. for fun

    b. for exercise

    c. to examine the nest closely

    d. to pick the beautiful flowers

9. Why did the snake wrap around Larry?

    a. It wanted a closer look.   b. It was cold.

    c. It was startled.   d. It wanted to climb higher.

10. What have we learned about jungles from this story?

    a. There is little rain.

    b. Temperatures are usually low.

    c. Few insects live in them.

    d. There are many dangers in them.

11. Why did Amanda lead the emergency party?

    a. She was always the calmest one of the explorers.

    b. She was the only one who knew where Larry was.

    c. She was the oldest and the smartest.

    d. Her job with the explorers was to act as a guide.

12. Why was Dr. Stewart lowered into the pit on a rope?

    a. to lasso Jimmy

    b. to tie up the boat

    c. to help himself get back out

    d. to tie up any snakes he found in the pit

B Almost every paragraph has two or more details that support a main idea. Read the following sentences and phrases. Label each **Main Idea** or **Detail**.

Example:

_____Detail_____ a. high humidity

_____Detail_____ b. high temperatures

_____Detail_____ c. crowded trees and bushes

_____Main Idea_____ d. a rain forest or jungle

_____Detail_____ e. many noisy birds

_____Detail_____ f. many insects

_____Detail_____ g. brightly colored flowers

1.

_____ a. the Amandamum

_____ b. long, slender buds

_____ c. pale, yellow color

_____ d. lovely flower when open

_____ e. eats insects

_____ f. has fragrance that attracts insects

2.

_____ a. The explorers brought in their supplies on burros.

_____ b. They brought food, tents, clothing, books, dishes, tools, computers, and typewriters.

_____ c. The explorers brought cameras, photographic supplies, tape recorders, and cassettes.

_____ d. Everything that was necessary for life had to be brought into the jungle by the explorers.

_____ e. They brought medicine, medical supplies, and cleaning materials.

Read the paragraphs below. Underline the correct main idea for each.

1.	Plants and animals cannot exist without water. They must drink it. People need it for bathing, cooking, cleaning, growing crops, and for pleasure. Water helps spread seeds and is an important means of transportation for humans.

   a.	Water is necessary for some living things.

   b.	Water is necessary for all living things.

   c.	People can travel on water.

2.	Most lizards that live in forests are green or yellow. Those that live in deserts are dull red or brown. Jungle lizards are brightly colored.

   a.	Lizards' coloring blends with the colors of the places where they live.

   b.	Lizards are colorful so that people will admire them.

   c.	Jungle lizards do not have as many enemies as desert lizards.

3.	Snake is the favorite food of mongooses. They almost always defeat snakes in battle. Mongooses attack by biting the back of the snake's neck. Sometimes a mongoose holds the snake's jaws shut so tightly that it is helpless. When the snake is too tired to fight, the mongoose eats it.

   a.	Mongooses enjoy eating snakes, but they can seldom kill them.

   b.	A snake can usually escape by waiting until the mongoose is tired.

   c.	Mongooses kill and eat snakes.

4.	An emerald boa lies on a tree branch in a strange way. It seems to be tied in a fancy knot that is higher in the center. On the sides its body is in loops. The boa's head is found in the middle of the knot. When a victim approaches, the boa unties itself rapidly and strikes suddenly.

   a.	The emerald boa is not a poisonous snake.

   b.	The emerald boa's victims are monkeys, lizards, and birds.

   c.	The emerald boa can surprise its victims by hiding on tree branches.

5.	Crocodiles and alligators choose a dry, sunny spot close to the water for a nest. The mother makes a large pile of dirt, grass, and leaves. She lays eggs in the heap and covers them with more grass and mud. The mother guards the eggs by lying on them most of the time. She only returns to the water for food. Other crocodiles lay their eggs in sand. The female digs a hole and deposits the eggs in the pit. The eggs are then covered well with more sand.

   a.	Some crocodiles and alligators have nests in water or on land.

   b.	The mother alligators and crocodiles leave their nests unguarded.

   c.	The nests of alligators and crocodiles are always built on land.

The sentence that tells the main idea of a paragraph is called the topic sentence. The topic sentence can be found anywhere in the paragraph. Read the following paragraphs. Find the topic sentence and underline it in each paragraph.

1. What a struggle it was just to walk through the rain forest. There were no roads or paths through the thick trees and bushes. Weeds, sometimes covered with thorns, grew high. Twisted vines hung from trees like heavy curtains. The explorers had to cut or push their way through.

2. The explorers found several huge tarantulas in the forest. Tarantulas—very large, hairy spiders—are dangerous to man and beast. Their size allows them to attack birds and other small animals. Tarantulas bite victims. Even adult human beings can become ill from the bite of these spiders.

3. To be a fish, a creature must have fins, gills, and a backbone. A starfish has gills but no backbone or fins, so it is not really a fish. Since a whale has no gills, it is not a fish. A jellyfish has no fins, no gills, and no backbone. Is a jellyfish really a fish?

4. First, Mom pulled out an old yo-yo with a twisted string. Next appeared a small but very hairy comb. Then, out came several scraps of wrinkled paper and some coins stuck together by a piece of old bubble gum. Laundry day always gave Mom many surprises when she cleaned out Amanda's pockets. But even she was amazed this time when she discovered a dead, smelly frog wrapped in a sock.

5. Most animals like to be left alone. They build their nests and homes in places where they won't be disturbed by enemies. It is also important that they protect their homes and families from nature. Strong winds, rain, and sun are troublesome to most animals. Animals usually live close to their food so they can eat and then retreat to their homes safely.

Skills Review (Stories 1–5)

 Read the article below. Note the details. Underline the topic sentence or main idea in each paragraph. Then answer the questions.

Sunflowers

1.   In a garden with many kinds of flowers, the sunflower will always be the first one noticed. That is because it is very tall. It can sometimes reach ten or fifteen feet in height. Each long stem is topped by a huge flower.

2.   The sunflower head is shaped like a very large daisy. The petals are usually yellow. They are all around a center, which can be black, brown, yellow, or purple.

3.   In the morning, when the sun rises in the east, sunflowers face that direction. At noon they raise their heads to the sun directly above them. When the sun sets in the west, the sunflowers are facing west. Sunflowers always face the light.

4.   Many birds eat sunflower seeds. Cardinals especially enjoy them. In some countries, the seeds are pressed to get the oil out. The mashed seed is then used to feed cows, horses, goats, sheep, and oxen. Sunflower seeds are very useful. The oil is used in making candy, salad oil, and margarine.

5.   Scientists in the United States have been experimenting with sunflower oil. They have been mixing it with diesel fuel and using it to run tractors. So far, the tractors can run only for a short time with the new gas mixture. The farmers and scientists hope they will soon be able to make it work better. Everyone would like to have cheaper, better fuel for cars, planes, ships, and tractors.

1. What is the main idea of the fourth paragraph? Write the topic sentence.

_____

_____

2. Which paragraph tells some uses of sunflowers? Underline the correct answer.

   a. paragraph 4   b. paragraph 2   c. paragraph 3

3. What is the main idea of paragraph 5? Underline the correct answer.

   a. Sunflowers are very tall.

   b. Tractors run well with sunflower oil.

   c. Scientists experiment with sunflower oil.

   d. Sunflowers have pretty petals.

4. What is paragraph 2 mainly about? Underline the correct answer.

   a. sunflowers facing the sun

   b. using sunflower oil in tractors

   c. the appearance of sunflowers

   d. the uses of sunflowers

5. Which is the best title for the whole article? Remember that the name of the story should tell what the article is mainly about. Underline the best title.

   a. Sunflowers for Cattle

   b. Facing the Sunrise

   c. How To Make Cardinals Happy

   d. A Useful Giant

   e. The Experiment With Sunflowers

B   **Read the following article. Then follow the directions on the next page.**

1.   Because of the daily showers and the high temperatures, rain forests are crowded with many types of plants. The vegetation is more varied in a rain forest than in any other region. There is a constant battle for space, light, and food among all the leafy residents.

2.   The plant life of rain forests exists in many forms. Trees that tower above the other plants form a leafy cover that cuts off most of the sunlight from lower plants. Vines spread and climb up the tree trunks to try to get their share of sun. Some plants are *air plants* that grow directly on other trees. They do not get food from the trees on which they dwell. They obtain food and moisture from the air. Palms and ferns grow closer to the ground. They can survive with little light. All these plants are evergreens.

3.   There is much competition for space, food, moisture, and light. If there are too many of one kind of plant or animal, some must die. Smaller and healthier numbers of each type of animal or plant can exist by competing with other species. The great variety of living things in the rain forest is only possible if there is a correct balance of living things.

4.   Humans tend to think of rain forests as fertile places where farmers can easily grow crops. But farmers must cut down sections of rain forests to make fields. It is only after their plantings fail that they realize the truth. The rain forest soil, after millions of years of constant growth, is thin and lacking in minerals and nourishment. When the jungle is intact, the soil is kept richer by everything that dies. The humid, warm weather helps the dead things decay rapidly. Rotted matter makes a layer of rich soil for plants. Cutting the normal vegetation to make a farm wipes out the supply of dead plants and animals necessary to keep the earth producing.

Draw lines to match each paragraph to its main idea.

Paragraph 1

Paragraph 2

Paragraph 3

Paragraph 4

a. Growth of the plants in the rain forest depends on how much light they need.

b. Farming has enriched the soil in the rain forest.

c. The climate of the rain forest helps many different kinds of plants to grow.

d. Farming is not successful in the rain forest.

e. Only a few of each kind of plant can exist in the rain forest.

Read the article below. Then shorten the information by outlining it. Some parts have been done for you. Use the Topic and Subtopic Box and the Additional Information Box to help you complete the outline. Skim the paragraphs if you need help.

The Tree Destroyer

The yellow-bellied sapsucker is a kind of woodpecker. It has a yellow stomach and its wings and back are black. The back has white spots, and the wings have white patches. The sapsucker's bright red head and throat make it very colorful.

Because of its eating habits, this bird sometimes destroys trees. Its favorite foods are birch and maple trees. The sapsucker drills a hole in the tree trunk. It drinks all the sap and goes back for more as the tree develops new sap. Simultaneously, sapsuckers eat the delicate tissues between the bark and the wood of the trees. These tissues form the rings that show the age of the tree, and destroying them often kills the tree.

Sapsuckers also eat insects, especially ants. While in the air, they consume numerous flies.

The nesting habits of the sapsucker can also damage trees. It pecks a gourd-shaped cavity in the tree to form a nest. The female lays four to six glossy white eggs in the nest.

Topic and Subtopic Box
Black back and wings
Lays four to six glossy white eggs
Catches flies in midair
Yellow stomach
Makes a gourd-shaped cavity
Eats insects
Food

Additional Information Box
Eats tissues between the bark and the wood
Drills a hole in the trunk
White wing patches

(Title of Outline) _____

   I. Appearance

       A. _____

       B. _____

           1. White spots on back

           2. _____

       C. Bright red head and throat

  II. _____

       A. Favorite foods—birch and maple trees

           1. _____

           2. Eats all the sap

           3. _____

       B. _____

       C. _____

 III. Nesting habits

       A. _____

       B. _____

This circle graph will help you learn what percent of people died from attacks by these poisonous animals during one year. Study the information on the graph. Then answer the questions below.

Deaths Due to Poisonous Bites or Stings

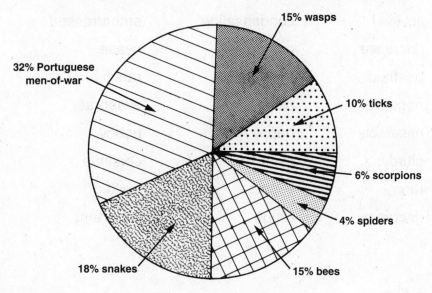

15% wasps

10% ticks

6% scorpions

4% spiders

15% bees

18% snakes

32% Portuguese men-of-war

1. Which poisonous animals caused the most deaths?

   _____

2. Which two poisonous animals caused the same number of deaths?

   _____

3. What is the difference between the percentage of deaths caused by snakebites and the percentage caused by bites of ticks?

   _____

4. What is the difference between the percentage of deaths caused by spiders and the percentage caused by wasps?

   _____

5. What two causes of death make up 50% of the total number?

   _____

6. List the poisonous animals from the most harmful to humans to the least harmful.

   a. _____   b. _____

   c. _____   d. _____

   e. _____   f. _____

   g. _____

Circle two antonyms in each group of words below.

1. experiment   contract   dissolve   expand
2. tension   inquired   replied   forgery
3. miserable   uncooperative   strange   familiar
4. liquid   condensation   embarrassed   unashamed
5. decrease   crease   cease   increase
6. unafraid   frightened   rare   solid
7. negative   positive   evaporate   complain
8. miserable   happy   hobby   photograph
9. sturdy   moist   continue   dry
10. rare   expert   trusted   undependable
11. decrease   rough   important   gentle

Place the dates below on the time line in correct order. Then read the dates and information in order so that you will have a better idea about America's history.

1836—Fall of the Alamo

1492—Columbus came to America.

1918—World War I ended.

1607—Jamestown was founded.

1969—People landed on the moon.

1776—Declaration of Independence

1941—Pearl Harbor was attacked.

"Help!" screamed Jimmy as his body continued its swift descent in the deep pit. His only thought was that he would be smashed on the bottom. The fall seemed to take forever!

Instead, he plunged into water! The water rushed along quickly, turning him over and over. Jimmy was a strong swimmer, but the water pushed him along so rapidly he was helpless.

He felt himself bump into rocks. It was too dark to see anything. Just as he realized that this river was under the ground, he was pushed out into bright sunlight. The force of water still carried him.

Jimmy grabbed a rock, hung there, and looked around. He was frightened. Just around the bend ahead, the rapids reached a sharp drop. The river went over the drop, forming a high waterfall.

The rapids tore at Jimmy. He could hardly hang onto the rock. His fear grew. Would he be swept over the waterfall?

Suddenly, the force of the current moved the rock! Jimmy was tossed about like a bouncing ball. Overhead he saw a dead tree hanging over the rapids. If he could get closer to the side of the river, perhaps he could grab the tree as he was swept by.

Only an excellent swimmer could fight against the strong current. Jimmy never understood how he did it. But there he was at the riverbank.

Worn-out but thankful, Jimmy was able to grab the dead tree. It was some time before he could force his tired muscles into action again. He wanted to pull himself out of the water, but he could not.

Little by little, though, he pulled himself out. Slowly he crawled along the tree, hugging it. Finally, he was on land!

Meanwhile, the search party had found where the underground river flowed out into the jungle. But the winding water was hard to follow in the rain forest. The group had to stop to beat through the bushes to see if Jimmy had been washed up on the bank. The search took hours.

Jimmy took a long rest on the riverbank. When he awoke, he smelled a fragrant perfume. Months of searching for the Mysteria made it a habit for him to trace all odors. Like a bloodhound, he had to decide where the fragrance was strongest. He followed the scent as it became more powerful. It came from a dark cave in the rocks behind the waterfall.

Before going into the darkness. Jimmy removed his torn shirt. He ripped it into several pieces. He tied the pieces to trees to show the path he was taking in case his friends found his trail.

"I'm glad they made us wear bright orange shirts," he thought.

Jimmy felt his way through the small cave, following the scent. At the far end, he saw light. Squeezing through a tiny opening, he came out into a meadow. It was the first open space he had discovered in the rain forest.

What an unbelievable sight he saw! Millions of lovely Mysteria flowers stretched before his eyes. The odor was overpowering. Each blossom had large, curly petals in shades of blue and purple. Jimmy had never seen such beautiful flowers before.

"The perfume makers will be happy about this discovery," thought Jimmy.

Being a young scientist, he cautiously picked one flower and broke its stem. Inside he found an oily liquid that dripped out slowly. This was the cure for a rare disease!

Later, the flowers would be picked to take back to the United States. The flowers would be photographed, too. Seeds would be collected to try to grow Mysterias in other countries. But meanwhile, carrying a large bunch of fragrant Mysterias, Jimmy retraced his path to the riverbank. There he waited for the search party to find him.

 Underline the correct answer to each question.

1. What is the best title for this story?

   a. The Discovery of the Amandamums

   b. Learning To Swim the Rapids

   c. Success by Accident

   d. Waterfalls and Caves

2. Which happened last in the story?

   a. Jimmy waited for the search party.

   b. Jimmy was in a river.

   c. Jimmy held onto a rock.

   d. The rock was swept away.

3. Why did the explorers wear orange shirts?

   a. They blended with the shadows.

   b. It was Dr. Garcia's favorite color.

   c. The color stood out in the jungle.

   d. The color matched the vines and bushes.

4. Which of these words means the movement of water?

   a. riverbank   b. current   c. realize   d. bounce

5. Why does the story describe Jimmy's actions as "like a bloodhound"?

   a. He acted like a dog.   b. He was following an odor.

   c. He was panting.   d. He was wild and upset.

6. What happened next after Jimmy grabbed the dead tree?

   a. He went into a cave.

   b. The dead tree broke.

   c. The rapids swept him away.

   d. He crawled on the limb and held on.

7. How do you think the search party will find Jimmy?

   a. by going back to camp for a map of the rain forest

   b. by using bloodhounds to track him

   c. by taking pictures from a helicopter

   d. by looking carefully on both sides of the river

8. Why did Jimmy rip his shirt into pieces?

   a. to leave a trail for the others to follow

   b. to dry himself after being in the water

   c. to give to the birds to build nests

   d. to make himself feel cooler

9. Why was it so difficult for Jimmy to swim to the bank of the river?

   a. He was a poor swimmer.

   b. He was in the rapids and currents.

   c. His injuries prevented strong swimming.

   d. He was injured when the dead tree toppled on him.

10. What was this story mainly about?

   a. how waterfalls are formed

   b. how to swim in the rapids

   c. a boy who could think for himself

   d. following a jungle trail

B Write all the words from below that mean the same or almost the same as a smell or to smell or to take in air.

_____ Word Box _____

cent	sniff	stink
expect	odor	breathe
current	sent	swift
fragrance	inhale	descent
muscles	scent	aroma

1. _____ 2. _____

3. _____ 4. _____

5. _____ 6. _____

7. _____ 8. _____

C Find a word from below that is a synonym for the underlined word or words in each sentence. Then write each sentence using the new word.

Word Box

swiftly	tossed	over
tracked	plunging	helpless

1. The swimmers were <u>diving</u> into the river.

_____

2. The current of the river moved <u>quickly</u>.

_____

3. <u>Above</u> him Jimmy saw a dead tree.

_____

4. He was <u>thrown around</u> like a bouncing ball.

_____

5. The bloodhound <u>followed the trail of</u> the lost camper.

_____

 D The main idea of a paragraph is usually told in the **topic sentence.** All the other sentences in the paragraph should give **details** or facts that support the topic sentence. Read these paragraphs. Underline the topic sentence of each paragraph. Then find one or more sentences in each paragraph that do not support the topic sentence. Draw a line through them.

Insects

1. Insects live in almost every kind of place. A few insects live in the sea, but most insects are found in fresh water or on land. Insects fly, crawl, hop, jump, walk, and swim. Insects live in the mountains, in deserts, in jungles, and in hot springs. Even in the ice and snow of the Antarctic, insects have been found. Insects can be different sizes and different colors.

2. All insects have two antennas, or feelers, on their heads. All have six legs and are covered with a waterproof material called chitin. There are more insects in the world than all other animals put together. The bodies of all insects are divided into three parts—the head, the abdomen, and the thorax. All insects have these things in common.

E Many times the title of an article or a paragraph will tell the main idea. Read each paragraph below and then choose the best title for it from the box. Write the title over the article.

_____ **Title Box** _____

Some Famous Waterfalls	Handle With Care
A Stubborn Animal	Kinds of Waterfalls
How Waterfalls Are Made	A Useful Animal

_____

1.   Waterfalls are beautiful sights to see. Some are unbelievably lovely because the water drops for very long distances. Others are lower but wider and have huge curtains of water streaming down. A few, great waterfalls are both wide and high.

_____

2.   A waterfall is a stream of water that drops freely over a cliff. It is formed when water flows over hard rocks first and then over softer ones. After thousands of years, the softer stones are worn down by the water. When the soft stones are gone, the water keeps on flowing, but over an empty space.

_____

3.   Burros are a kind of donkey. Because they are strong and healthy, they can do much hard work. Neither heat nor freezing cold bothers them much. Unlike human beings, burros seldom seem to get sick. They can carry heavy loads for long distances, climb mountains, and cross deserts.

_____

4.   Though burros are good workers, they cannot be trusted to do so on their own. They are often tricky and want to do things their way. If an owner does not tie a burro when leaving it, the animal will just walk away and never return. The owner is left without transportation. The clever burro learns quickly what its owners want it to do. Then the burro tries in every way to do just the opposite.

Some words have more than one meaning. Study the meanings of the two words. Read the sentences. Then decide which meaning fits each sentence. Write the correct letter of the meaning in front of each sentence.

bank

a. a place to save money
b. rising ground bordering a body of water

current

c. a movement of electricity
d. in general use; generally accepted
e. a flowing, onward motion; a stream, especially the fastest part of it

_____ 1. The *current* swept the boat down the stream.

_____ 2. The *current* style is to wear jeans.

_____ 3. A hippo stood on the *bank* of the stream.

_____ 4. She got a shock when the *current* came through the fallen wire.

_____ 5. He put the money he earned in the *bank.*

_____ 6. A *bank* will cash the check.

_____ 7. The crocodile walked down the *bank* and into the lake.

Read the following paragraphs. Then answer the questions about the main ideas and the details.

Cecropia Moth

Viceroy Butterfly

1. Every part of the body of a moth or butterfly has a special purpose. The thorax is made up of three sections. One pair of legs is attached to each part. The front wings are attached to the middle part of the thorax. The rear wings are attached to the back section. Under the covering of the thorax are found the muscles that control the movement of the wings and legs.

2.   The heads of moths and butterflies, like the heads of humans, have important uses. On the head are located the large eyes that stick out. They are compound eyes. That is, they are made up of many smaller sections to allow the insect to see in more than one direction at the same time. In this way, the insect can spot an enemy approaching from any direction. On the head are also found two antennae. They enable the butterfly or moth to smell and touch. The moth's antennae are feathery. The butterfly's antennae are like thin threads. These are ways to tell a moth from a butterfly.

3.   Color is more important to butterflies and moths than to any other animals. This is because butterflies and moths see colors. Cats, dogs, and some other animals see everything in shades of gray. Moths and butterflies see more colors than human beings. If flowers look lovely to you, they probably are more beautiful to a butterfly.

4.   Besides seeing in color, moths and butterflies have bodies covered with color. This makes it easy for males and females of one kind to find each other. It helps them to spot a butterfly or moth of a different type moving in on their territory.

5.   The colors on the wings are in spots, dots, and other patterns. In the air, these designs help conceal the insects from the sight of their enemies. The broken areas of color are even more important when the insects are resting. The colors provide protection. This allows the moths and butterflies to blend with their surroundings. In this way, moths are different from butterflies, too. Moths rest with wings stretched out flat so spots are found only on the tops of the wings. Butterflies rest with wings that are closed and held upright. Their bright color markings must be both on the top and bottom of the wings.

1. What is the main idea of paragraph 2? Write the topic sentence.

   _____

   _____

2. Which paragraph tells about the importance of the thorax? Underline the answer.

   a. paragraph 3   b. paragraph 2

   c. paragraph 4   d. paragraph 1

3. What is the main idea of paragraph 5? Underline the answer.

   a. Insects see colors of objects around them.

   b. Colors on wings of butterflies and moths are formed in dots.

   c. Colors protect these insects while flying and resting.

   d. There are three differences between butterflies and moths.

4. What does paragraph 3 mainly tell about?

   a. which colors butterflies like

   b. that butterflies blend with their surroundings

   c. that colors are seen by butterflies and moths

   d. that cats do not see colors

5. Match the correct title with each paragraph. Write the letter for each title next to the correct paragraph number.

   _____ 1.   a. How Animals See Colors

   _____ 2.   b. Colorful Protection

   _____ 3.   c. The Head and Its Parts

   _____ 4.   d. Bodies Covered With Color

   _____ 5.   e. What's on My Thorax?

6. Which is the best title for the whole article? Underline the answer.

   a. Nap Time for Insects

   b. Colorful Facts About Colorful Amphibians

   c. What Are You Picking Up on Your Antennae?

   d. Colorful Facts About Colorful Insects

Another Point of View

When Jimmy stumbled into the meadow of Mysterias, he did not know that he was being observed. The residents of the meadow concealed themselves noiselessly. But they watched the strange creature closely. "Was it a new enemy?" they wondered.

In the dense underbrush around the meadow lived a colony of birds the world had not yet discovered. The birds were gleaming dotted parakeets. Their spots were very bright, and the colors varied. No two birds had the same pattern or combination of colors. They had the usual parakeet shape and the small hooked beak, but the head was much larger. The head was larger to provide space for a brain bigger than that of any other bird in the world.

Yes, these birds were intelligent. They could think clearly and swiftly. They had learned to understand the languages of the other animals about them. They did not realize, because they had never seen a human being, that they would be able to understand human languages, too. These clever birds could also write! Here are some pages from the diary of Cedric Parakeet. Read them and be ready to answer some questions.

September 5—For months I have had no thoughts to record in my diary, because life has been dull. Our old enemies, the plaid owls, have not even attacked us lately.

We have enjoyed a huge crop of the seeds we love from all these blue and purple flowers around here. The yellow berries we enjoy are also in good supply this year. We parakeets have nothing to do except open our beaks and let the food roll in. Some of us have wings so unused to flying that our muscles are growing weak.

Today, however, something exciting happened. In the afternoon, a new creature stumbled into the meadow. It must be a bird, because it walks on two legs like us. It does not have wings, however, and it doesn't seem able to fly. When it first arrived, the creature rushed to the purple and blue flowers and sniffed them. Then it picked one. It broke the flower in half along the stem. When I saw the sap oozing out, I wanted to yell, "Stop! That juice is dangerous! It makes your skin sting."

September 6—I informed my wife, Zinnia, that I am really worried about the strange two-legged creature that just moved in.

"The bottom half of the creature has some strange covering," I said. "It's certainly not feathers. Perhaps it's fur. The top half is naked skin. The sun here in the meadow is very hot. The animal is beginning to get sunburned. How can I make it understand that it must crawl into the shadows?"

Zinnia flew to the edge of the meadow and looked at the creature. "I think it just hatched out of an egg," she announced. "Just wait. Pinfeathers will soon grow out of its skin!"

September 7—The two-legged creature must have learned about the effects of the hot sun. It stays in the shadows more now. At times it goes through the cave to the rain forest. How strange that it remains there for hours. The rain forest is shadowy, damp, and clammy.

I buzzed over the creature today and eyed its skin closely. No pinfeathers are growing yet!

When I told Zinnia, she said, "Speaking of feathers, you'd better start to build a new nest. We need it for the eggs I'm planning to sit on soon."

September 10—I had to neglect my diary for two days. Collecting feathers, strings, grass, and mud to build a parakeet nest is difficult work. Zinnia would not use the stringy stems of our local vine! No, indeed, only the stringy vines and stems of the morning glory flowers in the rain forest are good enough for her!

With all this flying about toting materials, I was completely exhausted. I was forced to neglect watching the odd two-legged creature. I did see it for a moment in the rain forest, sitting on the riverbank. I wonder if it found something good to eat in the mud there. Perhaps it eats insects and worms. It has not grown any pinfeathers yet!

September 11—Today the two-legged featherless bird saw me for the first time. I was admiring my new nest. Zinnia has been sitting on three tiny eggs since yesterday. I was busy bringing her some delicious yellow berries for lunch. I will confess that in my haste, I was a wee bit careless. The creature must have seen me carrying berries into the tangle of vines. The first thing Zinnia and I knew, a gigantic flipper pushed back the vine leaves. A tremendous face hung over our nest. I could see plainly that there were no pinfeathers sprouting on that face yet. But the head did have some thin black strings growing on the top and down the sides.

"It's all your fault, Cedric!" screeched Zinnia. "It followed you and found us. Now it will eat us!"

My wings turned to jelly. We would all be eaten—Zinnia, the eggs, and I! Then how surprised we were! The tremendous mouth opened. Words came out! We could understand every word. How could it be? We had never heard this creature before, but we knew everything it said.

"Well!" shouted the strange animal. "What beautiful parakeets these are, covered with spots of brilliant color! You're more lovely than butterflies or flowers! I wish I had my camera. When the search party comes, they'll want to photograph this unusual sight."

"What's a camera?" I chirped. "What does *photograph* mean?"

It was then that I discovered that this two-legged creature did not know what I was saying. It could not understand us even though we could tell what it was saying.

September 12—Zinnia is still sitting on the eggs. The strange animal still has no pinfeathers. It hangs around Zinnia and me when it is not in the rain forest. Mostly it lies under our vine and stuffs its mouth with berries and bananas.

Zinnia and I get nervous when it stands in the underbrush. It is weird to see those tremendous, brown eyes suddenly peering into the nest.

"How are the babies?" it always inquires politely. "Are they pecking their way out of the eggs yet?"

Zinnia always replies, "They're not ready to hatch," even though the creature cannot understand. "It takes three weeks for them to emerge."

It loves to talk to us. The words pour out. That pink tongue flaps and flaps!

"I've been here one week," the creature complained to us. "I got here on September 5. Today, September 12, makes a week. Will the search party ever find me?"

By now he has realized that we understand him. We nodded our heads "yes."

September 13—The creature wants Zinnia and me to go with him when the search party arrives. We did not nod our heads this time.

September 14—The large creature has its uses. It put its huge flipper over the nest and kept the eggs warm so Zinnia and I could go to visit our relatives.

September 15—We love our overgrown, featherless bird! Yesterday the plaid owls arrived, mean and hungry. One had already grabbed Uncle Todhunter in its talons when our creature interrupted. It used a broken branch to beat off the enormous owls. It caught Uncle Todhunter when the plaid owl's talons dropped him, too. But now Zinnia and I cannot even get near the creature! All our relatives are sitting on its head, flippers, and shoulders.

September 16—It happened today! The search party came! They ran into the meadow like a herd of water buffaloes. They looked just like our bird. First, they hugged our creature and screamed, "Jimmy!" What's a *Jimmy*? Then they ran through the field of blue and purple flowers, sniffing and smiling. After that they started breaking stems.

September 17—The creature showed us off to the search party. How undignified we were, hanging all over Jimmy. We were all there, except Zinnia, of course. She was still sitting on the eggs.

"I can tell the parakeets understand every word we say," announced Jimmy.

"They must come home with us. They're the most beautiful birds ever seen," a woman exclaimed.

"They're the most intelligent, too!" Jimmy added.

September 18—We found out what cameras are yesterday. We learned the meaning of *photography*. All morning the new creatures took pictures of Zinnia on the nest. They even gently lifted her to point the camera at the eggs. They photographed my friends and relatives. I made them snap the side of me with the pink and aqua dots.

September 19—Some other parakeets have decided to go home with the humans, as the creatures are called. Zinnia and I will not, of course. We are still waiting for the eggs to hatch.

September 20—Here I am all alone on the nest. All the other parakeets are in the rain forest, chirping farewell to the humans.

Wait! I hear that old, familiar crashing through the bushes. It has to be clumsy Jimmy! I knew it! Here come the big, brown eyes! What's he saying?

"I hope you'll come to live with me. We will wait until your babies are born. You were so good to me, and I want to give you a nice, safe home."

Flattery always wins me over. Zinnia, our little ones, and I will be going to a new home.

 Underline the correct answer for each question.

1. What does the title of the story, "Another Point of View," mean?
   a. The story explains how different Jimmy and the explorers appear to some birds.
   b. It means that the world looks different near a waterfall.
   c. It means that Jimmy changed his mind about exploring the rain forest.
   d. The story explains how birds watch everything humans do, so they can become more intelligent than people.

2. What made these parakeets different from all other parakeets?
   a. They could attack and kill owls.
   b. Their feathers had pretty colors.
   c. They could understand human languages.
   d. They built nests in vines.

3. What were the blue and purple flowers?

   a. berries

   b. Mysterias

   c. parakeet tulips

   d. Amandamums

4. Which of these was an enemy of the parakeets?

   a. proud owls

   b. calico cats

   c. plaid owls

   d. dotted snakes

5. Which of these materials were not used to build Cedric and Zinnia's nest?

   a. mud and feathers

   b. feathers and grass

   c. strings of morning glories

   d. leaves and hair

6. Where did Cedric observe Jimmy sitting and waiting?

   a. on the bank

   b. in the cave

   c. in a tree

   d. next to the plaid owls

7. What were the black strings on Jimmy's head?

   a. vines

   b. thorns

   c. hair

   d. feathers

8. Why did Cedric's friends and relatives love Jimmy?

   a. He fed them.

   b. He showed them where the yams were growing.

   c. Jimmy could understand what they were saying.

   d. He rescued them from danger.

9. What did Jimmy do when he acted as a baby-sitter for Zinnia?

   a. He sat on the eggs in the nest.

   b. He fed and cared for the baby birds.

   c. He kept the eggs warm with his hand.

   d. He carried the nest around with him.

10. What could Jimmy not do?

    a. talk to the parakeets

    b. understand the parakeets' language

    c. wait for the search party

    d. eat the berries growing around the meadow

B **Choose words from below to solve the crossword puzzle.**

___ Word Box ___

chirp	Cedric	swift
colony	excellent	depart
combination	haste	tote
contraction	juice	tube
dense	purple	twitter
exhausted	provide	varied

Across

1. to supply
3. the parakeet that kept a diary
4. very thick
6. a hurry
8. tree sap
10. a color
11. a bird's noise
12. to carry

Down

2. different each time
5. very tired or worn-out
7. to leave
9. the sound of a bird

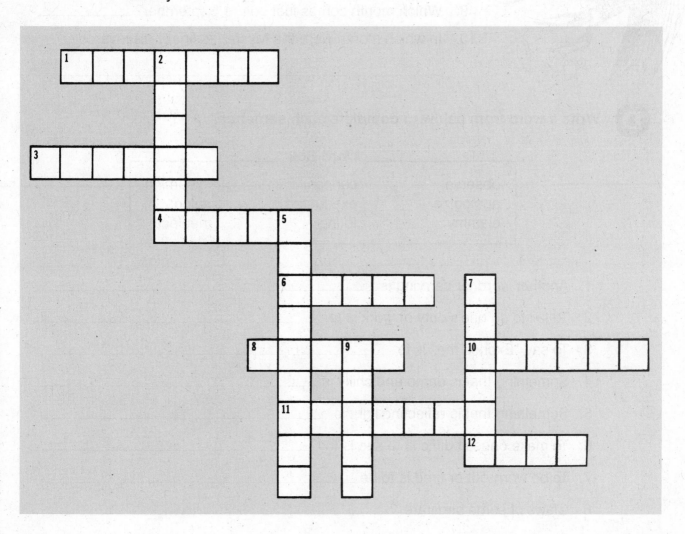

71

C   **Think, skim the story and diary entries, and use a calendar to answer these questions.**

1. How many days are in September? _____

2. How many days was Jimmy in the meadow before the search party found

    him? _____

3. How many weeks was that? _____

4. How many days does it take for parakeet eggs to hatch? _____

5. In what month will baby birds emerge from Zinnia's eggs?

    _____

6. Around what date will the eggs hatch? _____

7. When did Jimmy chase away plaid owls? _____

8. On which day was Jimmy a baby-sitter? _____

9. Which month comes just before September? _____

10. In which month were the Mysterias finally discovered?

    _____

D   **Write a word from below to complete each sentence.**

__ Word Box __		
observe	conceal	gleaming
apologize	exhausted	talons
clammy	toting	neglect

1. Another word for carrying is _____ .

2. To fail to do one's duty or work is to _____ it.

3. To say, "Excuse me," is to _____ .

4. Something that is damp and chilly is _____ .

5. Something that is reflecting light is _____ .

6. To make oneself difficult to see is to _____ .

7. To be worn-out or tired is to be _____ .

8. Claws of some birds are _____ .

72

Here I am again—Donna, the detective. This case started with a letter from my grandmother.

Dear Fellow Detectives,

I have positively the wildest mystery to solve. I can hardly wait to get started on it myself. I knew that, of all my grandchildren, you and Nick would most enjoy working out this puzzle with me. I will expect you the day after school closes for vacation. We will have a great time investigating this *super mystery* together.

I expect to hear from you no later than next week. Hurry! Hurry!

Eagerly,

Grandma Faye
Faye Taylor

P.S. Oh yes! You may bring your mother and father with you.

When we visited Grandma, she told us this story. One of her closest friends, Mrs. McIntosh, had died a few months ago. Because she had no relatives, Mrs. McIntosh left everything in her apartment to our grandmother. The two of them had been very much alike. They loved mysteries and solving puzzles. Mrs. McIntosh's lawyer told Grandma that there was a treasure hidden among the old books, furniture, china, paintings, clocks, and other antiques. He was supposed to start Grandma off on her search.

"She said that hunting for treasure would keep you from missing her too much," the lawyer told Grandma.

Grandma chuckled, "That sounds like Marge. What a sense of humor she had!"

Mr. Clark, the lawyer, said, "I have some clues here that Mrs. McIntosh left for you. But I enjoy mysteries, too. If you need help with these, please call me."

He had handed Grandma a paper. It was headed *Hints.*

HINTS
1. **Never throw away anything.**
2. **The most worthless might in the end become the most wonderful.**
3. **Happy sleuthing, dear fellow clue chaser.**

Grandma wanted to start the project right away. Mr. Clark gave us the keys to the apartment.

Mrs. McIntosh's apartment was in a big old house. Nicky and I were amazed to see how large the rooms were. They had to be large because they were stuffed with furniture and antiques of all kinds.

"Where do we start?" I asked. "In mystery books, the detectives always search through the desk first."

The only trouble was that Mrs. McIntosh had three desks—one in the living room, one in the bedroom, and another in the kitchen.

Mom suggested, "Look at this living room desk with all the pigeonholes. Desks like this often have secret drawers or cabinets."

"Okay, Mom!" exclaimed Nicky, darting toward the desk.

We took everything out of the desk and looked it over. We tapped the wood, measured, pushed, and pulled. But we found no clues or secret hiding places!

After lunch, we returned to the kitchen desk. It had one large drawer, which was empty.

Dad suggested, "Let's look at the back of the desk."

It took three of us to pull the desk away from the kitchen wall. As we struggled with it, my knee hit the wooden back. Suddenly a secret door popped open. There I finally discovered our first clue and an antique brooch.

The clue was on a tiny roll of paper. When Mom spread out the paper, we read a rhyme.

Hickory, dickory, dock,
The mouse ran down the clock.
The clock struck one.
The mouse was done!
But you're not through
Because here's a clue!
That mouse did not roam.
It went straight back home!

"The grandfather clock!" exclaimed Grandma. "That's the place to search next."

"We'll start there tomorrow morning. It's late now, and I'm tired," groaned Mom.

The next day, Grandma said, "I've been thinking about that rhyme. It told us that we were reading a clue and that the mouse went home."

"A mouse's home is a hole somewhere," decided Nicky.

I remembered something. In cartoons, the mice always popped out of holes in the baseboard. So Nicky and I crawled all around the rooms, studying the baseboards. We did not notice anything unusual. But behind one of the beds, we finally found it. A neat little circle was drawn on the white wood. Inside the circle were written the words, "the resident rodent."

First we shoved the bed aside. Then we removed the baseboard. Behind it was an opening. In the opening Dad discovered a small leather bag containing four gold coins and another slip of paper.

"These are from Marge's coin collection!" declared Grandma. "I guess she wanted me to have them."

"There's another rhyme on the paper!" I exclaimed. I read it aloud.

So you got this far
And won another clue.
It shows thinking on your part.
Good for all of you!
Now keep on going
Until you reach the gate.
Swing it back, swing it forth,
Before it is too late.

We searched, but no one could see anything that resembled a gate. Then Mom had an idea. "Perhaps it's an error. She may have meant grate."

All eyes turned to the fireplace. We all felt around in the ashes and up the chimney. Mom even climbed on Dad's back and up into the chimney. An hour later, my filthy ash-covered family had not discovered the hiding place.

I lay exhausted on the floor staring around the room. "I've got it!" I shouted. "There's a gateleg table in here." I pointed to a thin table against the wall.

When Dad and Nicky pulled the table into the center of the room, we took turns swinging the gatelegs to and fro. Gateleg tables have extra folding legs that can be pulled out. Then the top of the table unfolds and rests on these legs. It changes a small table into one much larger, around which several people can sit. But that still did not help.

"Turn the table upside down!" ordered Grandma. "Then move the gatelegs."

What a smart detective Grandma was! There was a small space behind each leg. From one space Grandma pulled a folded piece of paper. In another space was a plastic bag with a pair of gold earrings! Everyone had to examine the earrings. It was quite awhile before anyone looked at the note.

Dad was the first to notice. He said, "Hey there's something hard wrapped in this paper!"

Grandma had the honor of unfolding the note. Inside was a strip of metal that looked like this:

"What is it?" we all wondered.

Grandma read the note.

> It's in the room
> Not far from you.
> Look all around
> For an *obvious* clue.
> Use what you found—
> The thing's a key
> To open a lock
> Of something you see.

Everywhere we looked were locks and keyholes on drawers, on desks, on doors, on chests, and on boxes. It was too late in the day to try them. We decided to go home and try again the next day.

(to be continued)

Underline the correct answer for each question.

1. What type of story is this?
   a. It is a mystery.
   b. It is a collection of real facts.
   c. It is a fairy tale.
   d. It is a biography.

2. What had Grandma done to show she needed Nicky and Donna?
   a. She planned a big party for them.
   b. She did not search for the treasure without them.
   c. She invited all their cousins to meet them.
   d. She had presents waiting for them.

3. What kind of person do you think Mrs. McIntosh had been?
   a. thoughtful and fun-loving
   b. thoughtless and fun-loving
   c. jealous of other people
   d. unwilling to share with others

4. What was the third place in which a clue was found?
   a. the clock   b. the desk
   c. the fireplace   d. the gateleg table

5. Which of these words means *clearly seen* or *understood*?
   a. exhausted   b. obvious
   c. resident   d. resembled

6. Why did Mrs. McIntosh arrange this game?
   a. to puzzle the lawyer
   b. to give Donna and Nicky practice
   c. to keep Grandma from missing her
   d. to be sure Grandma got exercise every day

7. What do you think a gateleg table would have?
   a. a hidden gate   b. fewer than four legs
   c. more than four legs   d. extra drawers

8. Which of the following shows the correct order of places in which clues were found?
   a. the kitchen desk, the clock, the hole in the baseboard, the gateleg table
   b. the kitchen desk, the gateleg table, the hole in the baseboard
   c. the gateleg table, the kitchen desk, the hole in the baseboard
   d. the kitchen desk, the hole in the baseboard, the gateleg table

9. How did the circle get on the baseboard?

    a. A mouse chewed it.

    b. Mrs. McIntosh drew it.

    c. Grandma planned it.

    d. It was part of the wood.

10. Which of these is a *rodent*?

    a. a cat

    b. a pigeon

    c. a mouse

    d. a buffalo

11. Why could they not find the secret door in the kitchen desk at first?

    a. The door was hidden in the side against the wall.

    b. The door was locked, and they had not yet found the key.

    c. They had to call a locksmith to force the door open.

    d. none of the above

B   **Some words have more than one meaning and pronunciation. Study the word below and its meanings. Then write the letter of the correct meaning of the word next to each sentence.**

    project: a. (prō jěct´) *v*: to throw or cast forward

               b. (prō jěct´) *v*: to stick out or over something else

               c. (prŏj´ ěct) *n*: a plan, job, or task

_____ 1. The roof *projects* over the windows on the top floors.

_____ 2. Work had just begun on the *project* when it was suddenly interrupted.

        _____ 3. The machine *projects* an image on the screen.

        _____ 4. The shadow of the eagle, *projected* on the snow, alerted the lambs.

        _____ 5. The shoes *projecting* from under the bench were covered with paint.

        _____ 6. Improving his work in fractions and decimals is Nick's latest *project*.

There are different ways you can compare one thing to another. Sometimes you can compare pairs of things to each other, too. When doing this, you need to think about how the first two things are related to each other. Then think how the next pair should be related to each other. Complete each sentence by circling the correct word.

Examples:

a. A *big circle* is to a *little circle* as a *big square* is to a *little square.*

b. A *shoe* is to a *foot* as a *glove* is to a *hand.* (You wear a shoe on your foot. You wear a glove on your hand.)

c. *Hot* is to *warm* as *cold* is to _____. (All the words are alike because they deal with temperatures. Which word that expresses temperature would fit in the comparison and make sense?)

   oven   (cool)   snow

1. Medicine is to cure as poison is to _____.
   snakes   kill   drink

2. Hot is to cold as safe is to _____.
   harmless   safety patrol   dangerous

3. Roar is to lion as hiss is to _____.
   boy   snake   elephant

4. Bee is to hive as bird is to _____.
   nest   sing   wings

5. January is to winter as July is to _____.
   spring   summer   fireworks

6. Hunter is to jungle as fisher is to _____.
   boat   water   line

7. Time is to clock as temperature is to _____.
   winter   swimming   thermometer

8. Venom is to snake as sting is to _____.
   bee   pain   butterfly

9. Artist is to paint as chef is to _____.
   stove   engine   stone

The next day, we could hardly wait to begin our treasure hunt again.

Finding what the key opened was a tiresome job. The strange object fit none of the keyholes and locks in the furniture.

At last, Mom sat down wearily. "This is ridiculous. If we need information, instead of guessing we should go to an expert."

I replied, "The library can help us."

"Better yet, before going to the library, let's go to an antique store!" exclaimed Grandma. "Then we will have something to guide us in our search later at the local library."

An hour later, we were entering the second antique store. In the first, no one there had been able to identify the odd key.

The owner of this shop smiled as she heard our question. "I can't tell what the key fits, but I do know it is Oriental. There is a store near here that sells some Oriental antiques."

The owner of the next shop nodded his head as he looked at our key. "It unlocks a certain kind of Korean wooden box with heavy brass decorations. The lock is usually shaped like an animal and is very fancy. Somewhere on the lock will be a hole into which you push the key. It causes the whole lock to come apart."

Unfortunately, the owner had no boxes with locks of that sort to show us. So off we trekked to the library. Two hours later, we returned to the apartment loaded with books on Oriental boxes.

"I haven't seen anything around here that looks like any of these," I complained.

We looked high and low, in and out. This time our eagle-eyed mom spotted it. She was examining a corner table with a marble top. The three wooden legs were spread apart on the floor, but they got closer together as they neared the tabletop. Sneaky Mrs. McIntosh had slipped the Korean box into a space where the legs were close enough together to hold it. When seen from a distance, the box seemed to be a part of the table.

Now, was our suspense over? Would we finally see the treasure? Inside the box, everything was wrapped in an embroidered silk scarf. We unfolded the lovely material. There we found tiny figures of ivory and jade. One was an ivory figure of an ancient Japanese soldier with a sword. Another was a fat jade statue with a huge stomach. There was a Japanese fish of purple jade with curly fins and a huge grin on its face. Nicky's favorite was a tiny ivory octopus with eight curling tentacles and a puzzled expression. The one that made me shiver was a hideous ivory rat with a long tail.

"We haven't found a big treasure yet," said Grandma, "but we've acquired many small, valuable things."

At the bottom of the Korean box lay another poem.

> Look still further, my dear friend,
> The treasure hunt's not at an end.
> Go to where my coats do stay.
> This will lead you on your way.
> Look in! Look on!
> Look above! Look below!
> You will turn something
> Then you will know.

We made a mad dash to the hall closet. Dad, the tallest one, swept everything off the shelves. Grandma pulled out the few coats and searched them. Mom, Nick, and I went through the boxes, boots, umbrellas, and bags on the bottom of the closet.

"Nothing in this closet," I grumbled.

"We haven't found anything that turns," Mom said as she used the big wooden doorknob to shut the door. "Ooooh! I said that while I was turning this knob," exclaimed Mom.

Nick flew for a screwdriver. In no time, my handy little brother had removed the whole knob.

Grandma was the one who discovered that it was made in two parts. She and Dad had to tug in opposite directions until suddenly the wooden ball separated.

Out fell an emerald ring and still another one of those puzzling rhymes.

You've come so far
With each clue,
Yet you still haven't found
The best treasure for you.

It's on a place where
I've spent some time
Paying my bills
Or writing a rhyme.

Search for an object
That has something to tell.
If you can find it,
You'll be rewarded well.

Look it over,
Then get to the rear.
Don't give up!
Just please persevere!

Dad said, "Naturally, the place where she wrote rhymes and checks would be one of these desks. But which one?"

"We searched through all three of them," I recalled, "and we didn't find anything." There we were just where we had started, staring at three antique desks.

Again we pushed on carved parts. We pulled knobs, doors, and moldings. We tapped, rapped, banged, and knocked.

"It's fun to have a treasure hunt," said Nicky, "but it's upsetting when it takes so long!"

"We must persevere," warned Grandma.

I mumbled, "I'm not fond of any of this furniture, but this bedroom desk is positively the worst. It's so ugly with that clock built into the top. The clock doesn't even tick anymore. It's always 1:38." I stopped. A clock can tell something! I thought of the rhyme. *Search for a place that has something to tell. Hunt in the rear.* I shrieked! Dad was following my thoughts. He rushed for a ladder. I climbed up and tried to open the rear of the clock. I pulled on the cover, but it refused to budge.

"Press all the fancy carved flowers and leaves!" said Grandma. "Maybe there's a hidden button that will open it."

I was so excited I almost fell off the ladder. I let Grandma take my place. She leaned her hand for balance on a design in the wood. Click, the clock swung out! Behind it were three drawers. In the center drawer was a cassette.

Our excitement was unbelievable! What fun it was to solve a mystery! We gathered by Mrs. McIntosh's cassette player. It was on a small table beneath a large painting. While Dad switched on the player and slipped in the cassette, Mom admired the painting.

"This is really lovely!" she exclaimed to Grandma. "If you don't want this painting, please let us have it."

"I think it's beautiful, too," answered Grandma.

The painting was of a woman in a yellow silk jacket trimmed in white fur. She was standing near a window, arranging a bowl of flowers. Sunlight poured in the window to make the flowers, the lady, and her clothes gleam. The room behind her was in shadow. We could see an old map on the wall and a table covered with a heavy Oriental rug. But the lovely light on the scene made the colors glow.

Unexpectedly, Nicky spoke up. "I'm usually bored when we go to museums. But there's something about this picture that makes me want to stare at it."

Everyone agreed. Then Dad switched on the cassette player. As Mrs. McIntosh's voice rang out, we were astonished!

You have found it, my friend, Faye!
You're great with puzzles, I always did say.
Here's a priceless painting—yours to keep;
So are the furnishings and every antique.
This lovely picture is worth the most;
Of its beauty you can certainly boast.
Enjoy the colors, the figure serene—
It's the work of an artist not often seen.

"Here we were just admiring this painting," exclaimed Grandma, "and it turns out to be the great treasure!"

"It can't be that valuable," said Dad.

"Perhaps something is hidden behind the picture," suggested Mom.

Dad lifted the painting from the wall. Seen closely, the painting appeared to be quite old. The paint had tiny cracks in it. Dad cautiously removed the frame and the backing. Nothing was concealed either behind the picture or in the frame. No one said a word. We just stood watching Dad put the painting together again.

"Now, we obviously have a treasure," laughed Grandma. "But what is it? I know that the greatest treasure that I received was the pleasure of working together with my whole family."

"It was fun!" laughed Nicky, as we all hugged Grandma.

Once at home, Donna decided to do some detective work to discover more about the beautiful painting. But she did not know where to start. She thought she might talk with some experts. But she feared many experts would not take time from their busy schedules to speak to a young girl. Finally, Donna prepared this list of experts.

 A Read the list carefully. Then follow the directions.

Possible Experts

her art teacher in school

her friend who was taking painting lessons

the man in the paint and wallpaper shop

the director of the city museum

the man who owned the art supply shop

a neighbor who collected oil paintings

the head librarian of the art library

---

1. Name the four experts you think might help Donna the most.

   a. _____

   b. _____

   c. _____

   d. _____

2. In what order would you advise Donna to go to these experts to discuss the painting? Start with the ones most likely to know more about painting. Write them on these lines.

   a. _____

   b. _____

   c. _____

   d. _____

The experts listened to Donna's description. They looked at photographs of the painting taken by Dad. Almost all of the experts had suggestions about artists who could have painted it. But without expensive testing, the experts could not be certain. All of them told Donna to check out their hints in other places.

The experts suggested she look for:
- artists who had lived in the 1500s, 1600s, or 1700s, judging by the lady's clothing
- artists from Belgium, Holland, and the Netherlands because the room in the background looked like one found in those countries
- oil paintings

Donna then went to the encyclopedia to look up information about the artists the experts had mentioned. In which volumes should she look?

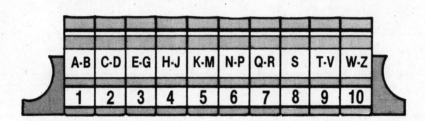

B **Think of topics Donna could look up. Write the information on the lines below. Use the headings given.**

	Volume	Letters	Topic
1.			
2.			
3.			
4.			
5.			

Here is a list of art books Donna looked at. Write five titles that might include the works of Belgian, Dutch, or Flemish artists who worked in the years from 1500 until 1750.

> **ART BOOKS**
>
> *Art In America*
> *The Best of French Artists: 1600–1800*
> *European Art and Artists*
> *A Guide to European Painters*
> *Famous Artists and Their Works*
> *Great Names in Art From the Fourteenth Century*
> *   to the Seventeenth Century*
> *Children of Famous Painters*
> *Great Masterpieces of the Netherlands*

1. _____

2. _____

3. _____

4. _____

5. _____

Art books have many pictures of paintings. Donna wanted to narrow her search to include only works by artists of the correct period and country. Of these, she wanted to read about artists who painted pictures of lovely ladies in home surroundings. She wanted to examine works only of the possible artists who specialized in pale, beautiful colors gleaming in sunlight. She also remembered Mrs. McIntosh's words that this painter's work was seldom seen.

Prepared with these clues, she tackled some thick art books. Because the tables of contents in them provided only general information and she did not want to read whole chapters, Donna had to use the indexes.

Here are some things Donna had learned about indexes.

1. The index is always at the end of the book.
2. The index is arranged in alphabetical order.
3. The index tells what topics are included in the book.
4. It tells how much information can be found on the topic.
5. It tells on which pages the information is located.
6. The index, like an outline, organizes the information under **main topics**, **subtopics**, and **details**.

 Here is a part of an index from an art book. Study it and then answer the questions.

Ancient art, 6, 9, 14, 35-270, 422-428;
  Byzantine, 35-41;
  cave drawings, 6, 9;
  early Christian, 14, 103-142, 422-428;
  Egyptian, 42-68, 70-89;
  Greek, 40-83, 85-98;
  Roman, 9, 84, 85, 98-142
Medieval art (years 900-1250), 307-637;
  architecture, 307-461;
    castles, 307, 311, 312-350;
    churches, 103-145, 308, 351-383;
  glass, stained, 422-426;
    illustration, 424;
  religious art, 360-475, 490-493;
  sculpture, 495-520;
    illustrations, 499, 518;

Renaissance art (years 1300-1700), 638-1058;
  Dutch, *see* Netherlands;
  England, 828-1018;
    painting, 866-893, 895, 899-910;
    illustrations, 870, 891, 900-905;
  Flemish, *see* Netherlands;
  Italy, 638-820;
    architecture, 602-620;
    murals, 811, 813, 815-820;
    painting, 684-691, 798;
    sculpture, 720-814, 819;
  Netherlands, 1062-1132;
    architecture, 1065-1089;
    map, 1063;
    painting, 1089-1132;

1. Which pages have information on medieval art? _____

2. Which pages have information on ancient Greek art?

_____

3. The period of Renaissance art is considered by this index to include

which years? _____

4. Give all the pages that have information about sculpture.

_____

5. If Donna does not find the information she needs in this book, what should she do? Underline the correct answer.

  a. not search anymore

  b. look in the index of another art book

  c. look in the table of contents of a book on sculpture

  d. search in the dictionary

After her research, Donna was sure the painting looked like the work of either of two Dutch artists from the 1600s. Whether it was real or a fake, she had no way of knowing. But a few months later, there was a notice in the paper. A famous art museum was sending some experts to Donna's city. They would examine paintings to decide if they were valuable. When they saw Grandma's painting, the experts knew it was rare and valuable. There was a mark at the bottom that the family had not noticed. That was one of the ways the artist had signed his pictures. So in the end, Grandma had a valuable treasure!

 Work out the acrostic puzzle on page 91 from the clues. The letters down the center will spell out the identity of a famous painter.

_____ **Word Box** _____

wearily	search	property
paint	ivory	protest
familiar	scarf	obvious
stranger	exclaim	antique
jade	shriek	persevere
either	object	Oriental
cousins	hideous	notice
	desk	

1. a kind of valuable stone
2. very ugly
3. to complain against
4. to cry out
5. one or the other
6. in a tired way
7. to keep on trying
8. to see
9. your aunt's son and daughter
10. a place to write
11. very old
12. a thing

90

13. to hunt or look for
14. to apply colors using a brush
15. plain to see
16. to scream or yell
17. the material an elephant's tusks are made of
18. known or recognized
19. something coming from Asia
20. something owned
21. a neck covering

1. __ __ __ __ __

2. __ __ __ __ __ __ __ __

3. __ __ __ __ __ __ __ __

4. __ __ __ __ __ __ __ __ __

5. __ __ __ __ __ __ __

6. __ __ __ __ __ __ __ __

7. __ __ __ __ __ __ __ __ __ __ __

8. __ __ __ __ __ __ __

9. __ __ __ __ __ __ __

10. __ __ __ __ __

11. __ __ __ __ __ __ __ __ __

12. __ __ __ __ __ __ __

13. __ __ __ __ __ __ __

14. __ __ __ __ __

15. __ __ __ __ __ __ __ __ __

16. __ __ __ __ __ __ __ __

17. __ __ __ __ __ __ __

18. __ __ __ __ __ __ __ __ __ __ __

19. __ __ __ __ __ __ __ __ __

20. __ __ __ __ __ __ __ __ __

21. __ __ __ __ __ __

A Some words have more than one meaning and pronunciation. Study the word below, its pronunciations, and its meanings. Then write the letter of the correct meaning of the word next to each sentence.

object: a. (ob´ ject) n: a purpose, an aim, an end
              b. (ob´ ject) n: a thing; a person
              c. (ob ject´) v: to oppose; to protest against

I object! The library closes too early!

LIBRARY
HOURS
9:00 – 1:00

That is an object of beauty.

_____ 1. They *objected* to people walking across their lawn.

_____ 2. The *object* of the game was to score touchdowns.

_____ 3. The *object* of the project was to complete it in three weeks.

_____ 4. The hero was the *object* of everyone's admiration.

_____ 5. The teacher *objects* to having the students call out.

_____ 6. Improving her work in decimals is Angela's *object*.

_____ 7. There was a mysterious *object* in the brook.

_____ 8. The cats were loudly *objecting* to eating the stale food.

92

Here are two young researchers looking for information for reports. They each have a different topic. Look at the pictures to see what they are researching. Read the titles of the books that may help. Write the names of the relevant books next to each picture.

Books
---

a. *The Hook and Ladder Trucks*

b. *The Know Everything Encyclopedia,* Vol. 2 Ba–Ce

c. *Night Watchmen of 1700 to 1840*

d. *Modern Russian Coins 1917–1992*

e. *The Know Everything Encyclopedia,* Vol. 7 Lu–My

f. *Early Fire Prevention Measures 1680–1900*

g. *French Currency Since 1789*

h. *U.S. Sheriffs Until 1895*

i. *English Coins 1800–1914*

j. *The Fire Department Joke Book*

k. *Crime in the U.S. 1776–1886*

l. *History of Italian Coins*

1.

My topic is "European Money in the 1800s."

1. _____

2. _____

3. _____

4. _____

2.

My topic is "Fire and Police Protection in the 1800s."

1. _____

2. _____

3. _____

4. _____

5. _____

Here is part of an index from a book about ancient peoples. See if you remember how to locate information in an index. Answer the questions that follow.

1. On what pages would you look to find out about the kinds of metal objects made by the people of China?

   _____

2. How many subtopics are listed for *Hunting*? _____

3. Does this index give any information about laws relating to hunting

   seasons? _____

4. Which pages would you read to find the most information about life

   during the Stone Age? _____

5. What subtopic would you read to find out when people first began to

   make objects from metal? _____

6. On what pages will you find maps of the Near East? _____

7. Are there more pages of information about farming in early Europe or

   farming in the Near East? _____

8. Which would be the best page to start to read to get the *most* information about metal artwork of the Etruscans? _____

9. What pages might tell you the kinds of tools used by farmers during the Iron Age? _____

10. What is the third subtopic under *Hunting*? _____

11. What is the fifth subtopic under *Farming*? _____

12. What pages might tell you the kinds of tools used by hunters during the Stone Age? _____

 D Read the following article. Then shorten the information by outlining it. Some parts of the outline have been done for you. Use the Topic and Subtopic Box and the Additional Information Box to help you complete the outline. Refer to the paragraphs in the article.

Poisons from Plants

Dangerous plants can be found all around us, even in our homes. Some of the most popular houseplants are poisonous if the leaves are eaten. Philodendrons, hyacinths, mistletoe, and poinsettias are all poisonous.

There are many poisonous wild plants found in our gardens and lawns. The most common of these are poison ivy, poison sumac, datura, and wild mushrooms.

Poison ivy and poison sumac are found almost everywhere in the United States. Both grow on sand dunes and seashores and in deserts, forests, mountain areas, and damp swamps. All parts of these plants are poisonous. Just touching a part of one can cause blisters, red skin, and itching.

The datura is also called the jimsonweed or thornapple. Any part of this plant may be poisonous if it is crushed. Jimsonweed grows in all different types of climates in Canada, Europe, and the United States. The poison affects the victim's eyesight, causes nervous twitching, and causes the heartbeat to be irregular—to beat too quickly or too weakly. A large quantity of datura usually brings on unconsciousness and then death.

Eating wild mushrooms is one of the most common types of plant poisonings. It is difficult to tell the harmless, good mushrooms from the poisonous ones, as they often look alike. For that reason, people should eat only mushrooms purchased in stores. Humans are tempted to try the wild ones, however, because they spring up everywhere—in lawns, gardens, woods, parks, and by the sides of the road in North America and Europe. Poisonous mushrooms are dangerous. They cause violent illness and even death.

Topic and Subtopic Box	Additional Information Box
Leaves poisonous if eaten	All parts poisonous if crushed
The datura plant	Harmless and harmful mushrooms look alike
Poisonous wild plants	Philodendrons
Wild mushrooms	Large quantity causes unconsciousness and death
Poison ivy and poison sumac	Cause blisters, red skin, and itching
	Poinsettias
	Causes nervous twitching

Poisons from Plants

I. Poisonous plants in our homes

   A. Kinds

      1. _____

      2. Hyacinths

      3. Mistletoe

      4. _____

   B. _____

II. _____

   A. _____

      1. Found almost everywhere

      2. All parts of plant are poisonous

      3. _____

   B. _____

      1. Found in Canada, Europe, and the United States

      2. _____

      3. Affects eyesight

      4. _____

      5. Causes irregular heartbeat

      6. _____

   C. _____

      1. Found almost everywhere about us in North America and Europe

      2. _____

      3. Cause violent illness and death

E This graph shows the number of days some students at Jefferson School were absent due to cases of poison ivy. Study the graph and then answer the questions.

Days 0 ½ 1 1½ 2 2½ 3 3½ 4 4½ 5 5½ 6

Students

Amy	
Randy	
Melissa	
Ahman	
Dolores	
Thomas	
Carmen	
Juan	
Chen	
Grace	

1. What kind of graph is this? Underline the correct answer.
   a. line graph   b. circle graph
   c. picture graph   d. bar graph

2. What information does this graph give you?

   _____

   _____

3. How many children had poison ivy? _____

4. Who was absent the greatest number of days? _____

5. Who was absent the fewest number of days? _____

6. Which children were absent the same number of days?

   _____

7. How many days was each absent? _____

8. How many days does each block stand for? _____

9. How many days do three blocks stand for? _____

10. What is the difference in the number of days missed between

    a. Amy and Carmen?   _____

    b. Dolores and Grace?   _____

    c. Randy and Grace?   _____

    d. Melissa and Chen?   _____

    e. Ahman and Thomas? _____

11. How many days did Ahman miss from school because of poison ivy?

    _____

12. Who do you think had the worst case of poison ivy?

    _____

13. Counted together, how many days were Melissa and Chen absent?

    _____

14. Counted together, how many days were Randy and Chen absent?

    _____

F **Complete each sentence by circling the correct word. Remember to think about how the things compare or relate to each other.**

1. Pencil is to write as truck is to _____.
   kiss   wheel   drive

2. Lungs are to people as gills are to _____.
   monkeys   insects   fish

3. Clue is to hint as odor is to _____.
   scent   cent   food

4. Humid is to jungle as dry is to _____.
   mountain   desert   valley

5. Nephew is to niece as uncle is to _____.
   cousin   aunt   sister

This is a myth from the Asian country of Thailand. There in the water lived a sea princess named Maykala (Mā´ kă´ lə). Her father, king of the sea, loved her dearly. Maykala was beautiful and fun-loving. She liked to swim in the waves and tease the fish. Only when dark clouds covered the sky did she stop having fun and dive down to her father's castle.

One day the king of the sea called to Maykala and said, "Maykala, it is time for you to marry. I have chosen the great Lord Siva (Sĭ´ vȧ) to be your husband."

This made the sea princess unhappy. She wanted to splash in the cool blue-green water and swim with the silver fish. She liked the sunshine, which made her flash like crystal on the waves. But to please her father, Maykala agreed to marry Lord Siva.

Just before the wedding, the sea king gave his daughter a beautiful present. It was a crystal ball.

He said, "When you feel sad or lonely, polish the crystal ball. Then look into it, and you will remember your home and the good times you had with your friends."

Lord Siva married the sea princess and took her to his palace in the sky. Maykala loved the castle, and she made many friends. She dashed around and visited everyone.

One day as she wandered through the airy palace, she discovered she was alone. Only the guards, who were to watch and protect her, were there. A feeling of loneliness came over her.

She said to herself, "Oh! I wish I could go outside the sky castle! If I could only go past the palace gates, then I could play in the sun."

Maykala remembered her father's gift. She got the crystal ball and began to polish it. When she looked into it, she could recall the beautiful sea that had been her home in the past. The silver waves dazzled her eyes in the brilliant sunshine. She decided to take the crystal ball outside to collect all the colors of the rainbow in it. Then she would have memories of her present home reflected in the ball.

Quietly, she crept on tiptoe to the gate. She saw that the guards were asleep, so she rushed past them. She danced and skipped from one soft cloud to the next as she held the crystal ball. Maykala felt very happy and free in the warm air.

As she skipped along, Maykala became aware of a large dark shadow covering her. She looked up and saw an evil-looking giant glaring down at her. Dark rain clouds hung to his black cape.

"What are you doing here? Who are you, girl?" he snarled.

Maykala was scared at first. Then she thought that since she was the wife of the great Lord Siva, this evil-looking giant had no right to talk to her that way. Maykala said, "Who are **you** to talk to me that way?"

This made the giant angrier. He roared so loudly that he caused the clouds to shake and the wind to blow. Down on the earth, huge trees fell, and gigantic waves arose on the seas.

The giant roared, "I am Ramasoon (Rǎ´ mǎ sūn). No one dares to talk to **me** like that."

Maykala quickly danced to another cloud. Ramasoon, in his black cape that held dark rain clouds, raised his large ax to throw at the princess.

Maykala quickly pointed the crystal ball at the sun. The dazzling light from the sun reflected off the ball and flashed into the giant's eyes, blinding him. With a deep roar, he dropped his ax. It missed the princess and fell to the earth with a crash. Maykala laughed at the giant, which made Ramasoon even angrier. As he went down to the earth to pick up his ax, Maykala quickly danced to another cloud and waited for the giant to return.

Once again she flashed the crystal ball in his eyes, and once again Ramasoon yelled and threw his ax. But each time, he missed Maykala. In his great anger, Ramasoon let his black cape fly out behind him to free the dark clouds there. Then the rain poured down to the earth.

At this time, Maykala decided to stop playing games. She had had enough fun for one day. She returned to the castle and tiptoed softly into her bedroom. She dried her hair and then rotated her crystal ball so she could see all the colors of the rainbow glittering inside.

So, once a year all the gods in Lord Siva's castle leave to do their work. In the empty rooms Maykala is lonely. She escapes past the sentry and plays hide-and-seek with Ramasoon, the ugly giant. Every time she flashes her crystal ball in his eyes, he throws his ax at her. When the ax drops to the earth, Thailand's rainy season begins. Many storms lash the country.

The children of Thailand are never afraid of thunder and lightning. They know what is happening when they see lightning streak through the sky and hear the loud crash of thunder. Ramasoon, the ugly giant, is chasing Maykala, the lonely sea princess, across the heavens. And they know he will never catch her.

Underline the correct answer to each question.

1. What did Maykala's father give her for a wedding present?
   a. a black cape
   b. some silver balls
   c. a ball made of glass
   d. a large wedding cake

2. Where did most of this story take place?
   a. in the heavens
   b. in the rain forest
   c. on the sun's rays
   d. in the Atlantic Ocean

3. What kind of person was Maykala?
   a. She could tell the future by looking into her crystal ball.
   b. She was the goddess of all sea animals.
   c. She was a goddess who could cause the waves to roar.
   d. She was a playful sea goddess.

4. When did Ramasoon first throw the ax at Maykala?
   a. before she flashed her crystal ball at him
   b. after Maykala flashed her crystal ball at him
   c. at the same time that she flashed the crystal ball at him
   d. The story does not tell.

5. What power did Ramasoon have?
   a. He could make the sun and moon move in the heavens.
   b. He could make the sea princess do as he wished.
   c. He could push all the colors of the rainbow into a crystal ball.
   d. He could make rain and terrible storms.

6. What is the best title for this story?
   a. The Wedding of a Sea Princess
   b. How To Sneak Past Sleeping Guards
   c. Dancing on Clouds
   d. Why Thunder Follows Lightning

7. What kind of story is this?
   a. a true story
   b. a myth
   c. a biography
   d. a detective story

8. What happened when Ramasoon threw his ax?
   a. Rains fell.
   b. Thunder cracked.
   c. Winds roared.
   d. Lightning struck.

B Myths were made up many years ago. Early people tried to explain all the things they could not understand. They decided superhuman gods and goddesses caused and controlled all the events of nature and everyday life.

Here are some characters from myths of different lands. What facts of nature were early people trying to explain? Write the fact under the myth.

_____ **Facts of Nature** _____

what rainbows were
how sunshine on the waves made them glitter
what the stars were
what happened when winter came
how day and night came about
what thunder was

1. In Roman myths, Pluto, the king of the underworld, stole the lovely daughter of the harvest goddess. The world became cold and snowy. No crops could grow. What did this myth try to explain?

_____

2. In the Thai myth, Maykala was the daughter of the sea god. The ocean was her playground. As she danced and ran on the rippling waves, she flashed like crystal on top of the water. What did this myth try to explain?

_____

3. Helios was the god of the sun. Every day he drove his chariot across the sky, giving the world light. When he reached the end, he disappeared. However, he returned again each day at dawn to drive his chariot through the heavens. What does this myth try to explain?

_____

Match the correct effect to its cause. Write the letter of the effect beside its cause.

CAUSE	EFFECT
_____ 1. Because Maykala used to live in the water,	a. winds blew and waves arose on the seas.
_____ 2. Because the guards were sleeping,	b. she skipped from cloud to cloud.
_____ 3. Because thunder follows lightning,	c. they are not afraid of thunder and lightning.
_____ 4. Because Maykala's father was afraid she'd be lonely,	d. she was called the sea princess.
_____ 5. Because Ramasoon roared,	e. Ramasoon was blinded for a while.
_____ 6. Because Maykala wanted to dance,	f. she married Lord Siva.
_____ 7. Because Maykala pointed the crystal ball at the sun,	g. Maykala was able to sneak out.
_____ 8. Because Maykala wanted to please her father,	h. she left her home in the sea.
_____ 9. Because the children of Thailand know the myth of Maykala and Ramasoon,	i. he gave her a crystal ball.
_____ 10. Because Maykala married Lord Siva,	j. the myth says Ramasoon is chasing Maykala.

Underline the correct answer to each question.

1. What is *crystal*?
   a. something shining with fire inside
   b. a kind of princess
   c. a kind of glass

2. What does *recall* mean?
   a. to rewind
   b. to remember something
   c. to return something

3. What can *glitter*?
   a. a ring around a sink
   b. a diamond ring
   c. a telephone

4. What is a *sentry*?
   a. a shiny, new coin
   b. a package or bundle
   c. a guard

5. What is a *myth*?
   a. a lovely young animal
   b. an ancient tale
   c. a new movie

6. What can *reflect*?
   a. a piece of black cloth
   b. a cave in the ocean
   c. a piece of crystal in the sunlight

7. What does *loneliness* mean?
   a. having fun
   b. being without friends
   c. feeling jealous

8. What does *past* mean?
   a. a time in the future
   b. this present moment
   c. the time before now

11

This story was reported in newspapers around the world and on TV news programs several years ago.

Joe Crystal, 28, was a photographer working for *Daring Adventures Magazine.* One Friday the thirteenth, his assignment was to cover a skydiving event.

"I really didn't even want to get out of bed!" Joe has since claimed. "I was trembling from fright when I packed my gear and drove to the airport. I knew this was Adam North's thirteenth jump, and it was happening on Friday the thirteenth."

Crystal was to photograph the stunt divers from the local skydiving club. He and a pilot, Tracy Ortiz, planned to photograph the jumpers from the time they leaped from the plane until they landed safely on the field below.

Ortiz, 43, brought the plane close enough for Joe to follow the jumps of Lou Girard, Agnes Brent, Barbie Chin, and Bob Preston. They successfully completed some difficult stunts before opening their parachutes. Joe was able to take some color photographs from unusual angles. They are so clear that one can even see the different facial expressions of the jumpers as they fell.

Then came Adam North, 23, making his thirteenth dive. He had been skydiving for five years. In a moment of carelessness, Adam forgot to keep his body in the jumper's arch—legs, arms, and head back—as he leaped. Joe Crystal realized what was happening and kept his camera running as he followed the drama in the sky. On film, he caught Adam as he tried to open the parachute while tumbling the 3,600 feet toward the ground. The parachute's lines became tangled around Adam's legs. Next, the parachute wrapped around him like a plastic bag. From waist to toe, Adam was covered by folds of nylon. Joe's camera kept on filming.

"The other chute!" Tracy Ortiz was yelling over and over. Adam opened his reserve parachute. It, too, twisted around the sky diver. Joe Crystal groaned as the camera recorded the agony on Adam North's face.

By this time, Adam was falling at a great speed. He stayed calm, however. He tried to relax his body. Ortiz and Crystal shook their heads with pity. They were sure Adam was "a goner."

The camera recorded the stuntman rapidly falling toward a river. Now it was too dangerous for the photographer and his pilot to follow closely. But they did get a picture of Adam's plunge into the water, which was deep after two weeks of rain. The crowd dashed over and pulled Adam out. Joe and Tracy saw people jumping up and down in joy. Then they realized that the sky diver was alive.

An ambulance took Adam to the hospital. Adam had a broken leg and rib and bruised kidneys, but was in good shape considering the length of his fall. The photographer and his pilot won several awards for excellent reporting and photography. Adam North's award was the fact that he survived such a fall.

This event captured the interest of many people. A book was written about it. It was also made into a television program and into a movie. A number of magazine articles were written about it. All these versions said they were telling facts the way they happened. But some of them made up extra parts that were not true to add to the story. We call stories with made-up parts *fiction*.

Often you will be told a story is true when it is really fiction. You must check all the facts yourself. Then you will be able to tell whether the story that you are reading is *fact* or *fiction*.

You have read the story of Adam North. You know what is true. Now here are descriptions or parts of the television shows, the movies, the books, and the articles written about Adam. Read each one. Label each fiction or fact.

_____ 1. A movie called *The World Turned Upside Down*:

The director says, "This exciting adventure film tells the story of brave Joe Crystal and Tracy Ortiz, a photographer and a pilot, who are taking pictures of sky divers doing stunts. When a sky diver becomes tangled in his parachute, the clever pilot radios the airport for help. At the same time, he brings the airplane under the falling man. The two in the plane catch the falling sky diver! The pilot and the photographer manage the first midair rescue of a person! This film should pack in the audiences."

_____ 2. A book called *Free Falls*:

The publishing company announced, "This is a book of photographs taken over two years by Joseph Crystal. They are studies of the training and the work of sky divers. He shows every step in the teaching and practicing of this exciting and popular sport. The text accompanying these prize-winning pictures was written by Tracy Luis Ortiz, the pilot who has worked with Crystal in his study of sky divers. Ortiz, besides being a brave and skillful flier, writes clearly and beautifully. His reports make the reader live through the hopes, fears, joys, and sorrows of sky divers.

"The book includes pictures of the thrilling fall of Adam North, whose parachute did not work. Ortiz, a friend of North's, described his own feelings as he watched his pal drop toward what he thought would be North's certain death."

_____ 3.   A magazine article called *Great Escapes*:

This article tells the stories of nine people who narrowly escaped being killed in accidents. Laura Benson and Aiko Inichi, the only two survivors of a plane crash in Washington D.C., told the writers the strange story of their rescue. Adam North, who lived to tell the tale after he plunged to the earth, described to the authors how he felt when both of his parachutes failed to open.

_____ 4.   A television show called *The Sky's the Limit*:

On this program, skydiving and free-falling were described and photographed. The reporters visited several skydiving clubs and schools. They spoke to many teachers and students.

The photographers took pictures as a reporter interviewed Adam North, Tracy Ortiz, and Joe Crystal about Adam's famous fall. It was on this program that North first announced to the world that he would no longer be skydiving. The leg he had injured when he plunged into the river had not healed well. His doctors felt that the leg could no longer bear the strain of parachute landings.

B **Underline the correct answer to each question.**

1. How old was Adam North when he started sky diving?
   a. 22   b. 13
   c. 18   d. 15

2. For which magazine was Joe Crystal working?
   a. *Skydiving Journal*   b. *Viking Magazine*
   c. *Daring Adventures Magazine*   d. none of these

3. How many jumps had Adam made before the one written about in this story?
   a. The story does not say.   b. 12
   c. 10   d. 13

4. Why wasn't Joe Crystal eager to photograph this skydiving show?
   a. He didn't have all of his equipment.
   b. The weather report said it was going to rain.
   c. Friday was his day off.
   d. He was superstitious.

5. Why must sky divers carry a reserve parachute?
   a. to help the photographer take a more colorful picture
   b. to help balance the diver
   c. in case the first one does not work properly
   d. none of the above

6. Which of these happened first?
   a. The parachute twisted around Adam's body.
   b. Adam forgot the jumper's arch.
   c. Adam hit the water in the river.
   d. Joe and Tracy thought North was "a goner."

7. Why do you think Adam's parachute did not open properly?
   a. because he had forgotten his reserve chute
   b. because of careless packing of the parachute
   c. because there was no wind
   d. because Adam's body was not in the right position

8. Which of these best describes a sky diver?
   a. superstitious, calm, and quick-thinking
   b. fun-loving, honest, and trustworthy
   c. calm, brave, and quick-thinking
   d. strong, tall, adventurous, and neat

Many advertisements try to convince you to buy certain products, even if you do not need them or if they are not as good as other products. As the buyer, you must watch for these tricky ways of selling. These types of advertisements are called persuasive advertisements. Persuasive advertisements do not give much reliable information about the products being sold. Instead, they give this information:

Persuasive Ways of Selling

1. Some ads tell you that famous actors, singers, athletes, or rich people buy and use the product.
2. Some ads tell you that everyone else is buying the product. You should buy it, too, just to be one of the crowd.
3. Some ads tell you that there is a new, secret ingredient in the product that makes it better than anyone else's.

 Here are some newspaper, radio, and television ads. Read each one. Put a ✔ beside each ad that gives you the information you need to know about a product. If the ad tries to persuade you through tricks, write the number of the type of persuasive techniques.

_____ 1.

*Excitement and fun at home!
Enjoy hundreds of games!
Sports! Space monsters! Mazes!
Only $48.27.
Strong, well-made controls.
On-screen directions. Easy to operate.
One-year guarantee. Your money back
if not satisfied.*

_____ 2.

Six out of ten doctors recommend the Frizzee Electric Curling Iron. It's safe for any type of hair. Bonnie and Johnnie, famous singers, say, "Frizzee made us what we are today."

_____ 3. Are these snowy days giving you sore, red, chapped hands? Cheer up! Help is on the way. Eppiss Company is having a sale on all their gloves. Warm, leather gloves and mittens with silk, fur, or dacron linings reduced from $22.88 to $12.95. Beautiful, wool gloves, fully lined, reduced from $9.98 to $6.50. Sold at all fine stores.

_____ 4. At last the mystery of the Sphinx is told! From the mummies comes the secret of the ingredient that made Cleopatra so slim and beautiful— _Glexo-Vitaheva-Dorpokeloline_. Only _Slinky_ contains this magic ingredient that kills the extra calories you eat each day. Just eat, then take a _Slinky_. Everything else you eat for four hours does not count! Have you ever seen a fat mummy?

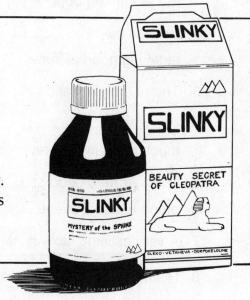

_____ 5. Can you afford to let your kids be different? Everyone's wearing the famous Zedoz Hyena shirts. In Europe, Australia, New Zealand, Japan, North America, and South America, 9 out of 10 of the "in people" proudly display hyenas over their hearts.

D Choose a word from below to complete each sentence.

_____ Word Box _____

bear	successful	gear
survivors	drama	reserve
description	recorded	publishers
persuade	plunged	superstitious

1. Those not killed in a crash are called _____.

2. A _____ person will
   not walk under a ladder.

3. The diver _____ into
   the swimming pool.

4. He was never _____
   at taking good pictures.

5. The photographer's
   _____ took up too
   much room in the car.

6. Tracy wrote a good _____
   of the unusual event.

7. A very exciting story is called a _____.

8. His friends were unable to _____ him to skydive.

9. The _____ printed two books about narrow
   escapes.

10. His leg could no longer _____ the strain of
    parachute landings.

11. The _____ club puts on two plays a year.

12. One _____ survived the forest fire.

Factual material can be proven true. The details can be checked in records or in the words of eyewitnesses.

Fictional material can be based on true facts. However, the author of fictional material might do some of the things listed in the box below.

If any of these are present in shows, movies, plays, or writings, they are fictional materials.

Here are some parts of stories. These authors did not intend to write fiction. Some of the authors, however, changed factual material into fictional material based on fact. Label each story **fiction** or **fact**. If the story is fiction, underline the details that changed fact to fiction.

- put in impossible details that do not fit the time period
- include impossible actions, events, or deeds
- make up characters that did not exist but that act, talk, and dress as if they could
- include conversations that no one can prove are the exact words spoken by the characters
- contain characters such as ogres, giants, elves, witches, plants, animals, and people that are unheard of in real life

_____ 1.   One of the most important dates in American history is July 4, 1776. On that date, the 13 colonies adopted the Declaration of Independence. The colonies at that time were ruled by England. For some time, one colonial group or another had wanted to gain freedom from England, but each group was too weak to break free alone.

_____ 2.   Only when the 13 colonies banded together did they have enough strength to challenge the British king. The colonists formed the Continental Congress, with representatives from each colony. These representatives met for almost a year to decide what course of action to take.

3.   After a year's work, the Continental Congress decided what to do. They wrote a declaration of why the colonies wanted their freedom. They told of unfair acts of England against them. They declared that no longer would they remain colonies. Instead, all 13 colonies would form an independent country.

    Thomas Jefferson wrote most of the Declaration of Independence. The ideas, however, were the result of work by him and others, such as Benjamin Franklin, Mickey Mouse, Ronald Reagan, and John Hancock.

4.   "Listen!" exclaimed Cyrus Lee. "The Liberty Bell is ringing!"

    Cyrus, a thirteen-year-old cobbler's son, lived in Philadelphia in 1876.

    "Hurry!" shouted his sister, Lizzie, running to the door of the small shop. "Come on! We will miss the reading of the Declaration of Independence!"

    The bell was calling everyone in town to come to the square to hear what their leaders had decided to do. Before joining the crowd, however, Cyrus and Lizzie had to lock the door of their father's shop.

5.   In Washington, D.C., you can see the Declaration of Independence. Some of the patriots scribbled when they signed their names. Their writing is barely legible. Others wrote very clearly. But John Hancock's signature is the largest and clearest on it.

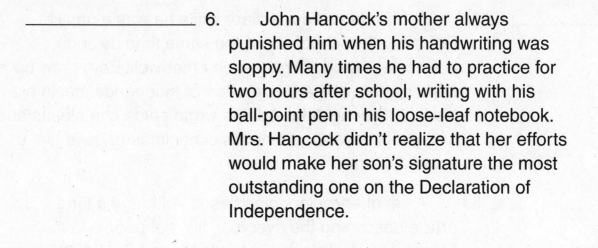

_____ 6. John Hancock's mother always punished him when his handwriting was sloppy. Many times he had to practice for two hours after school, writing with his ball-point pen in his loose-leaf notebook. Mrs. Hancock didn't realize that her efforts would make her son's signature the most outstanding one on the Declaration of Independence.

_____ 7. The Declaration was signed by 56 men, representing the 13 colonies. John Hancock was the president of the Continental Congress at the time. He and his brave fellow signers knew that this act would probably bring a war. They risked their lives, their homes, and their fortunes.

 If you wish to find information about John Hancock's school days at Boston Latin School, you can look in many places. Some of these writings below from books, stories, and articles are relevant, which means they are likely to contain true facts on that topic. Others are not relevant. They would not give information about Hancock's education.

   Write relevant in front of four of these references that you think may contain true material about Hancock's education. Underline all the material in the others that would make it not relevant to Hancock's education. One is done for you.

_____ 1. *Child's Day Magazine* published an article called "William Deering at Boston Latin School." <u>It is the true story of a man who was a pupil at the famous school in the years from 1904 to 1910.</u>

_____ 2.   John Adams kept a diary while he was a pupil at Boston Latin School about the same time as John Hancock. The boys knew each other well. Both grew up to be signers of the Declaration of Independence. In his diary, the young John Adams wrote some complaints about his school days. One time his schoolmaster gave him a sound beating.

_____ 3.   A set of encyclopedias has in Volume 4 a long article describing the everyday lives of people in the Massachusetts, Virginia, Maryland, and South Carolina colonies from 1700 to 1775.

_____ 4.   A book entitled *American History: Everyday Life in the Colonies* was published in 1812.

_____ 5.   A book entitled *United States History from 1850 to 1980* was published in 1982.

_____ 6.   A book called *The Lives of Infants and Children in English Colonies in America* was written by Mabel Sterling Davis in 1804. She was born in New York in 1774. Some of her family fought in the Revolutionary War.

_____ 7.   *Learning Can Be Fun Magazine* has three stories in each issue which tell exciting adventures about history. In the November issue are these three stories: "A Schoolboy of Old Wyoming"; "Beulah, a Girl of Colonial Georgia"; and "Fiona and Angus of Virginia."

_____ 8.   A book called *Education in the Colonies From 1500 to 1800* gives an outline of how children were taught. Famous colonial schools are described.

SKILLS REVIEW (Stories 10–11)

 A Underline the correct answer to each question.

1. Which did not *survive*?
   a. a house left standing after an earthquake
   b. a century-old stone wall
   c. a melted snowflake
   d. a fence surrounding a camp

2. Which of these is not *legible*?
   a. a perfectly written letter   b. a neatly typed article
   c. a hasty scribble   d. a well-printed newspaper

3. Which of these is *gigantic*?
   a. dazzling neon lights
   b. soft and mushy mushrooms
   c. microscopic water animals
   d. the enormous continent of Asia

4. Which of these is a *sentry*?
   a. a period of 100 years   b. a watchful guard
   c. an ocean   d. a delivery

5. Which of these means *snarled*?
   a. old and bent   b. trapped
   c. like a snail   d. growled and snapped at

 B Read the ads below. Put a ✔ beside each ad that gives you the information you need to know about a product.

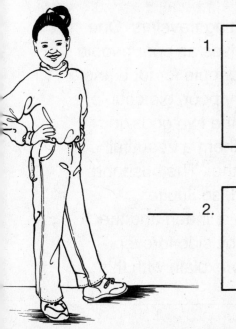

_____ 1. "Nothing can part me from my Tordack jeans!" says Sheila Jones, a top fashion model at the age of 13. Sheila's beauty has made her the one to watch for new fashion ideas. In her eighth-grade classes, you can always pick out Sheila. She's the one in the Tordack jeans!

_____ 2. Special! Two days only! The popular Aardvark shirts are now only $10 each. Made of fine cotton, these shirts are guaranteed, washable, and preshrunk. All sizes are available. Choose from frosty white, sunshine yellow, sky blue, emerald green, and shell pink.

Read the following myths. What facts of nature were early people trying to explain? Write the correct fact of nature under each myth.

┌─────────── **Facts of Nature** ───────────┐
│   │
│ creation of trees and bushes   │
│ why volcanoes erupt   │
│ what rainbows are   │
│ the seasons of the year   │
│   │
└──┘

1.   A giant displeased the mighty gods and goddesses.
They punished him by shutting him inside a high mountain.
Sometimes the giant struggled to free himself from his
prison. He shook the mountain and breathed fire and
smoke as he did so. What were the people trying to
explain? _____

2.   Jupiter was the Roman god protecting travelers. One
day he and Mercury disguised themselves as poor people
on a journey. They went about asking people for food and
shelter. Everyone refused except a very poor, old couple.
They shared everything they had with the two gods. In
return for their kindness, Jupiter gave them a beautiful
home and let them live a long life together. The husband
and wife never wanted to be separated, so Jupiter
changed them into trees. One became a linden and the
other an oak. The two trees grew side by side forever.
What were the ancient people trying to explain with this

myth? _____

Luke and Alice Wong are going to Thailand, a country in Southeast Asia. To plan their trip carefully, they will look up as much information as possible and speak to people who can help them. Answer the questions below.

1. Underline the people who may be able to give them relevant information about the journey.
   a. a librarian
   b. a guard in a museum
   c. a Japanese artist
   d. a clerk at the airline office
   e. a travel agent
   f. a musician who lived in Thailand from 1845 to 1940
   g. a friend who lived in Thailand from 1986 to 1999

2. Circle the letters of three references that might give them the most relevant information.
   a. *Thailand's Neighbors*
   b. *Travel in Asia on $50 a Day*
   c. *Atlas of Southeast Asia*
   d. *Recipes From Thailand*
   e. airplane schedules of Asia Airlines
   f. *Travel to Europe on $50 a Day*
   g. *Ancient Thailand*

3. All these people have written books. Which three authors would most likely give the Wongs relevant information? Underline the answers.
   a. Carol Ashton, a mechanic in Hawaii, who services planes from Thailand
   b. Thanom Petchaburi, the publicity agent of the Thai Tourist Center
   c. Pibue Chakri, who wrote *Life of a Thai Silkworm*
   d. Elena Cordoba, a writer who travels all over the world and reviews airplanes, hotels, and restaurants
   e. Nancy Gale, a geography professor, who writes for travel magazines

Mrs. Wong, who is an author, was in Thailand to study the everyday life of the Thai people. Here are some articles she has written. Read the titles. Write fact next to the ones that most likely contain factual material. Write fiction next to the ones most likely to contain imaginary material.

1. Living Near Thailand's Canals _____

2. All About Thai Giants and Ogres _____

3. Animals of Thailand _____

4. How Elephants Are Trained _____

5. The Life of the Thunder God _____

6. The Silkworm Speaks _____

7. Favorite Foods of the Thai People _____

8. The Climate of Thailand _____

9. How Thai Silk Is Made _____

10. Favorite Thai Myths _____

11. The Lobster That Swallowed a Thai Family _____

12. The Lumber Industry in Thailand _____